Don't Throw It Away

A. W. Coysh

David & Charles
Newton Abbot   London
North Pomfret (VT)   Vancouver

Books by the same author

The Antique Buyer's Dictionary of Names
Blue and White Transfer Ware 1780–1840
Blue-printed Earthenware, 1800–1840
British Art Pottery 1870–1940
Collecting Bookmarkers
Historic English Inns

ISBN 0 7153 7429 X
Library of Congress Catalog Card Number: 77–80148

Set in 11 on 13pt Linotype Baskerville and printed in
Great Britain by Latimer Trend & Company Ltd Plymouth
for David & Charles (Publishers) Limited
Brunel House   Newton Abbot   Devon

Published in the United States of America
by David & Charles Inc
North Pomfret   Vermont 05053   USA

Published in Canada
by Douglas David & Charles Limited
1875 Welch Street   North Vancouver   BC

Contents

Acknowledgements

For the loan of items illustrated in this book I am indebted to Lady Brightman, Miss W. Holloway, Mrs W. G. Marlowe, Mrs T. N. Taitt and Mrs R. G. Wells. The photographs were taken by Studio Wreford of Hungerford, Berkshire, with the exception of that on page 53 which is by courtesy of Associated News Group Ltd.

A. W. Coysh

Among Old Papers

Every year in Britain thousands of pounds' worth of goods are thrown away or destroyed because they no longer appear to serve any useful purpose. How many housewives today use a flat iron? How many men shave with a cut-throat razor or keep an inkwell on their desks? These are all bygones. Yet there are many people who would be delighted to have them and would get great pleasure from them. Indeed, some people would be prepared to pay good money for them.

Relatively few discarded articles are likely to fetch as much as a hundred pounds. There are, however, all manner of small bygones which sell readily – even Victorian items such as sugar crushers and glove stretchers – and many people wonder who creates the market for these oddments from the past. The answer is simple – collectors. There are clubs for collectors of bottles, caddy spoons, clocks, coins, costume, dolls and dolls' houses, ephemera (ie old advertisements and papers), fire-marks, furniture, glass, maps, matchbox labels, militaria, musical boxes, musical instruments, newspapers, pewter, pottery and porcelain, postage stamps, playing cards, pot lids, silver, watercolours, wine labels and many others.

When going through old papers people tend to spend too little time examining them. Printed matter including advertising material, trade cards and old greetings cards that have served their immediate purpose are usually thrown away. Relatively few survive. Victorian examples are hard to find and are now sought by collectors as 'printed ephemera' or 'transient printed oddments'. So, when looking through papers, see if there are any of the following among them:

Advertisements and Trade Cards
In the days before chain stores and supermarkets almost every small business took trouble to advertise its wares. For this

purpose trade cards were printed using a great variety of type-faces and sometimes attractive woodcuts to indicate the stock-in-trade. Old advertising leaflets and greetings cards or bookmarkers carrying advertisements should be saved. It is just possible that you might find an old poster although owing to their size they have seldom survived.

Banknotes and Charity Notes

Travellers abroad sometimes bring back paper money which they fail to exchange, or they may preserve British or foreign notes out of interest or as mementoes. Such banknotes are sought after, as 'notaphilia' is increasing in popularity. British notes are the most popular but foreign notes are also collected.

Banknotes have been issued in Britain since the reign of Charles I and by the end of the eighteenth century over 400 banks were printing notes. Many of these went bankrupt and by the middle of the nineteenth century most of them had ceased to issue notes. Some of these early notes can be worth a great deal of money. The 1869 £5 issue of the City of Glasgow, for example, has fetched over £1,000. Even the ten shilling and £1 Bank of England notes which carry the head of George V and are signed by Warren Fisher now fetch several pounds. It is also just possible that you might find an old charity note. These were issued by various charities and entitled the holder to a night's lodging or some other amenity. Watts's Charity of Rochester, for example, founded in 1597 as the result of a will left by Richard Watts, issued such notes in the eighteenth and nineteenth centuries. Banknotes were often hidden in a secret drawer in old writing desks.

If you find any old banknotes read about them before you dispose of them. There are several useful books on the subject:

Beresiner, Y. L. and Narbeth, C. *The Story of Paper Money* (David & Charles, 1973)

Narbeth, C. *Collecting Paper Money* (Lutterworth Press, 1968)

Narbeth, C. (Editor) *Collect British Banknotes* (Stanley Gibbons, 1970).

London dealers in banknotes include B. A. Seaby Ltd, Audley House, 11 Margaret Street, London W1N 8AT and All Change, 26 Pelham Road, London SW9. Most coin dealers buy old banknotes.

Billheads and Pictorial Writing Paper

Old bills are often kept longer than most ephemera as a record that they have been paid. Victorian examples are not uncommon and these have not only an attractive variety of lettering but, as with trade cards, they often carry an engraved print symbolic of the goods or service provided. A tea importer might perhaps show a clipper in full sail, a fruiterer a bowl of fruit, or a carrier a waggon and horses. I recently found a bill in an old book for an interment in 1848. It shows a view of the South Metropolitan Cemetery, Norwood, Surrey, when it had only two or three rows of graves. At a recent auction a cardboard box full of Victorian bills fetched £7 and was cheap at the price. Notepaper and envelopes in early Victorian times also carried attractive engraved views. Look out for these and preserve them.

Catalogues

Old sale and exhibition catalogues, and booksellers' lists can be of great interest to those who study antiques and bygones, particularly if they are based on fine collections and are illustrated. Exhibition catalogues often contain information about pictures, furniture, porcelain or other valuable antiques which is not available elsewhere and provide useful source books for dealers, collectors and museum curators. Auction-sale catalogues sometimes provide similar material if they list the lots in detail, and are of special interest if they describe the contents of an historic house or list private collections which are being dispersed. Trade catalogues of all kinds often help in the dating and attribution of goods no longer on the market. The Army & Navy Stores Catalogues, for example, contain so much valuable information that selected items from them have been reprinted in facsimile as *Yesterday's Shopping* (David & Charles, 1969).

Greetings Cards

The practice of sending Christmas and other greetings cards has only been well established for about a hundred years although Valentines were popular much earlier. It spread with the introduction of the half-penny post for cards and unsealed envelopes. Old greetings cards are now widely collected. They have a wonderful period flavour and those designed by well-known artists such as Walter Crane and his brother Thomas, who was Art Director for the publishers Marcus Ward & Co, are particularly valued. Undoubtedly the most successful artist in this field was Kate Greenaway, whose designs showing young children at work and play were immensely popular and now sell for considerable sums. If you are interested in old greetings cards, try to obtain George Buday's *A History of the Christmas Card* (Barrie & Rockliff, 1954 and Spring Books 1964), the classic reference book on the subject.

Invitation and In Memoriam Cards

Invitation cards to dinners, exhibitions and other functions usually have an interesting layout and a variety of type. *'In Memoriam'* cards (see p 17) are usually simpler but often have floral decoration. They are well worth preserving.

Labels

Labels are among the most attractive pieces of ephemera but are seldom found in good condition since they are usually attached to old bottles, packages or luggage. Occasionally un-used specimens turn up. Some time ago I bought a box of books at an auction sale which contained an old notebook of the 1870s in which a Victorian chemist had written down the recipes for his medicines and potions. Among the papers was his trade card and some of his bottle labels in mint condition (see plate 1). If you find one on an old bottle don't soak it off: it may disintegrate. In fact the bottle itself may well have an antiquarian interest. There are even collectors of modern labels: collections of cheese labels and wine-bottle labels have appeared quite recently in auction sales.

8

Luggage labels were more commonly used before the motor car became the chief means of transport. Shipping companies and hotel proprietors issued their own labels to travellers. Some were kept in mint condition as souvenirs while others are found on old trunks and suitcases, stuck there not only to facilitate delivery of luggage but also to impress friends!

Letters and Records

Old letters should be studied carefully. Do they throw light on historical events, on social conditions, or on the personalities of well-known people of the day? You may be in doubt about this. If so, each administrative county has an archivist whose job it is to sort through and preserve all kinds of documents. I have been asked to stress that no archivist minds dirt, ladders, or heavy loads: he or she is always willing to come and look!

It is just possible that when sorting through letters you may find one signed by an eminent author, musician, artist or statesman. These can be valuable.

Before the introduction of the penny post letters were simply folded and sealed with sealing wax. They were taken by mail coach and there will probably be some indication of the charge made for this. After the introduction of the postage stamp envelopes were generally used. Covers with early Victorian stamps or with early foreign stamps are sought by collectors especially if they have an interesting postmark. Letters posted at sea, for example, which bear the postmark 'Paquebot' are of special interest and even envelopes of 1918 and 1945 with the postmark 'Victory' are worth saving.

Business firms, professional men and societies all keep records of their affairs and sooner or later find it impossible to preserve more than they need for the current conduct of their affairs. Very often it is assumed that they can no longer be of interest so they are destroyed. In this way valuable information can be lost for ever. The British Records Association exists to safeguard and preserve all kinds of documents for posterity. Do not assume that a document is too recent to

9

be kept. In fact less is often known about the history of modern business firms than about those flourishing two centuries ago. Minutes, ledgers and daybooks should be kept in their entirety. Research reports, deeds, correspondence, manuscript maps, estate surveys and rentals, working drawings showing the construction of machinery, pattern books, catalogues, photographs of products, and many other papers may in future be of value to the social historian.

Menus and Wine Lists

These are of great interest not only for the style of printing and decoration but also as a reflection of the eating habits of the period and place. Sometimes they are signed by some of the diners and may have significant autographs. They are often treasured as mementoes of important occasions and are therefore found quite frequently among old papers. I recently rescued a whole set of well designed menus that had been kept as souvenirs of holiday cruises in the 1930s.

Music Covers

One day when viewing a house sale I found a bulky pile of sheet music on the floor beside the piano. It was a single lot but the room was so crowded with people that I found it impossible to sort through the sheets. When the auctioneer came to this lot he failed to get a bid until I offered 50p, and the pile was knocked down to me. Sorting out the music at home, I found a considerable number of pictorial sheet-music covers spanning a period from about 1880 to 1920. The rest of the music was worthless and went to a waste-paper merchant. Had the owners taken time to sort the music before sending it to the sale, the auctioneers would have been able to catalogue it in some detail and the material would probably have sold for between £20 and £30.

Pictorial sheet-music covers are collectors' items. Indeed, they are now reproduced, to be framed for wall decoration. Many of the covers were designed by first-class artists, especially those that were colour-printed. The earliest nineteenth-century covers were printed in black type using a great variety of type founts, differing for every major line with sweeping copper-plate scrolls and flourishes between them. In the 1840s the first hand-coloured lithographs began to appear, many designed by John Brandard (1812–63). (The artist's name appeared on the covers.) Then came the colour-printed lithographs. Between 1860 and 1900 many fine covers were designed. The most notable designer of this period was Alfred Concanen (1835–86), who not only produced some fine scenic covers but also many showing the great singing stars of the music halls such as George Leybourne and the Great Vance wearing the costumes they wore on stage. After the death of Concanen the finest designer was probably H. G. Banks, who produced covers for the type of music made popular by the Christy's Minstrels. By this time, however, music-cover art was in decline. There was a brief revival of colour printing in the 1920s and 1930s but for economic reasons the process used only two or three colours. Nevertheless, the designs are characteristic of the period and are also collected.

Many music covers are illustrated in Ronald Pearsall's *Victorian Sheet Music Covers* (David & Charles, 1972) and *Victorian Popular Music* (David & Charles, 1973).

Playbills and Programmes

Nineetenth-century playbills, usually long and narrow, were exhibited in windows to give publicity to visiting theatrical and music-hall companies. They are occasionally found folded in books or in folders of old papers. If you find one, treat it with care. The paper on which they were printed was usually flimsy. They should be smoothed out and backed with cardboard but do not stick them down. The whole can then be protected with a transparent covering. Usually they are worth framing for they are rare and have value. Those with the names of well-known actors and actresses of the period are, of course, the most sought after but they all have a social and historical interest. I recently rescued a playbill advertising theatrical performances given at the Assembly Rooms at

11

Newry, Northern Ireland, in 1863, by 'the Officers of the 58th Regiment in aid of winter clothing for the Poor of Newry', the main item being a play by Mark Lemon, one of the founders of *Punch* who was a prolific writer of melodramas.

However, you are much more likely to come across old theatre and concert programmes than playbills, for these are often kept as mementoes for sentimental reasons. They may be worth saving, particularly if they are souvenir programmes printed for a special occasion or, as quite frequently happens, they bear the autograph of a well-known artist.

There are many people who are interested in anything connected with the theatre – old tickets, prints, photographs and other relics. See J. K. Melling's *Discovering Theatre Ephemera* (Shire Publications, 1974).

Tickets

Relatively few tickets for travel or special events survive; they are usually surrendered at a barrier or entrance door. They are therefore of special interest to the collector of ephemera. I recently found a subscriber's ticket for the Edinburgh Institution for the Encouragement of Sacred Music in an old book. It is a beautifully engraved print dated 1819 and it is remarkable that it should have survived for over 150 years (plate 1). In another book I found a ticket for a bass singer to take his place in the mass choir at the British Empire Exhibition in 1924 and a transport ticket for two people to travel on the 'New Empress Saloon' from Southend to London. Save all old tickets.

Valentines

Long before Christmas cards were sent the Valentine was already popular. In the early nineteenth century letters were often written on embossed and decorated paper and then, early in the 1850s, lacy Valentine cards decorated with ribbons, flowers, gilding, and cupids were produced, sometimes with ingenious centres which opened out to display a message or figure behind.

Valentines were very popular indeed up to about 1870 when the Christmas-card trade expanded. As they were often kept for sentimental reasons, they have survived in surprisingly large numbers though seldom in mint condition. Unfortunately many Valentines were mounted in scrap albums and they are so flimsy that it is virtually impossible to release them without damage. Don't try. I recently saw an album of mounted Valentines sell for over £70.

Wartime and Crisis Ephemera

After a war or a time of crisis we are usually only too glad to forget the past and look forward to an optimistic future. As a result the things that remind us of bad times are destroyed. Official Ration Books are an example. Propaganda leaflets, documents, correspondence, airgraphs and other wartime documents are all worth keeping and so are petrol ration books.

Other Ephemera

Look carefully at any old certificates, proclamations, or printing concerned with elections. These may have historic interest. Having looked through your papers you may decide that there is nothing old enough to be of interest. However, collectors are already preserving ephemera of the 1960s and early 1970s which will be of interest to future generations. I have beef tokens, for example, issued in 1975 to old-age pensioners so that they could buy beef at a reduced price (plate 1). Most of these were cashed, so they are already uncommon. Preserve any material of this type, storing it in a dry, well-ventilated place. Remember, paper can be damaged by fungoid growths if kept in damp conditions, or even by animal or insect pests. Any paper stored away, including books, should be examined from time to time.

One of the most useful books on items described in this chapter is John Lewis's *Printed Ephemera* (Faber & Faber, 1962, paperback 1969).

The Contents of the Desk

A desk or lady's davenport will yield all kinds of writing materials and other oddments. It may also contain smoking accessories.

Writing Accessories

Inkstands

Almost every desk had a stand of some kind to hold inkwells. The commonest stand was made of wood with depressions to hold cut-glass inkwells, each with a glass lid fitted with a silver or brass hinge. The stand would also have a depression for the pen. Some would be more elaborate with a small paper-rack fitted to the back. A few even had clock or watch stands. Other inkstands were of brass or porcelain, sometimes with two matching candlesticks. The china stands usually had a small hole in which the pen could be placed. Surprisingly enough, there is still a demand for old inkstands. Don't throw them away, even if they are damaged. The wells or other parts may be used for restoration. Not long ago I saw two badly damaged wooden stands, each with one of the glass wells badly cracked, sell at auction for over £5. Wooden inkstands in perfect condition can reach double figures.

Paper Clips

In Victorian times pending accounts and other papers were often hung by a clip on the wall waiting for attention. For this purpose a strong sprung brass clip was used, often in the shape of a hand. The clips are usually fastened to a piece of varnished wood made to hang flat against the wall. They often bear a moulded registration mark, in which case they can be dated.

Paper Knives

In the nineteenth century and up to World War I, books were bound from folded sheets which were seldom trimmed as they are today. The sheets had therefore to be cut with a knife before the pages could be read. For this reason paper knives were everyday equipment, some being small enough to fit the pocket or fitted with a ring to be carried on a chain. Many were furnished with a clip so that they could also be used as book-markers.

Paper knives made of wood, bone, ivory, tortoiseshell, celluloid, silver and plate may be found. Some were printed with advertising material and given away by tradesmen (plate 2).

Paper knives were frequently made as souvenirs. The wooden example (plate 2) has a small transfer-print of Felix-stowe Beach, with bathing boxes and ladies in Victorian costume. Woodware of this type, including boxes, serviette rings, needle cases and other items, was produced extensively from about 1830, mainly by Smiths of Mauchline in Scotland. The trade expanded with the growth of the railway and the habit of taking seaside holidays. Articles carrying a local view were sold as souvenirs in every resort, and they were even exported. Their popularity was enormous as this was before the days of the picture postcard.

Paperweights

The most attractive of all paperweights are probably those bun-shapes of glass enclosing small pieces of colour which resemble flowers or butterflies. These were first produced in Italy and are sometimes called *millefiore* (or 'thousand flowers'). The most famous factories, however, operated in France, in the nineteenth century, at Baccarat and Clichy. The Baccarat weights have a letter B and the date (eg 1847) enclosed within the flowers. If you find one of these French paperweights you have something very valuable indeed. Some modern paperweights are already becoming collectors' items, especially those made in Scotland at Oban and Caithness.

Glass paperweights both bun-shaped and rectangular were made in considerable quantities as souvenirs in Victorian times. These usually have a small coloured print affixed to the base (see plate 2), or perhaps a photograph, usually of a seaside resort or a tourist attraction. They fetch a few pounds. Some souvenirs were made of alabaster (a material that is easy to work) with inset photographs protected by glass.

Metal paperweights were sometimes made in the shapes of animals such as boars, dogs and foxes. These sometimes have a felt inset which could be used as a penwiper. Do not confuse them with pincushions.

Pens, Penknives and Pencils

In the nineteenth century most letters were written with a goose or swan quill shaped with a knife, although after a time the feathers were abandoned in favour of a more rigid penholder, into which the short writing end of the quill could be fitted, and it was then possible to buy quills ready-cut. The spring-folding penknives which were kept on the desk for cutting quills have often survived. The commonest are the Sheffield-made knives with thin blades which were still used in the early years of the twentieth century (plate 2). Some intended for ladies were also fitted with scissors and button hooks. Penknives with scimitar-like blades were imported from France and these usually have tortoiseshell or mother-of-pearl handles.

In Edwardian days 'hand-cut goose nibs' could be bought in boxes. By this time, however, the metal nib had largely replaced the quill. Boxes of metal nibs are often found in desks and among boxes of old stationery. I recently acquired three boxes by accident when I bought a box of old papers and envelopes at a small auction sale. One box contains a selection of nibs by William Mitchell of London; another is filled with circular pointed nibs made by C. Brandauer & Co of Birmingham that 'neither scratch, nor spurt, the points being rounded by a new process'. The third is of 'relief' nibs by R. Easterbrook & Co, a firm which started making steel

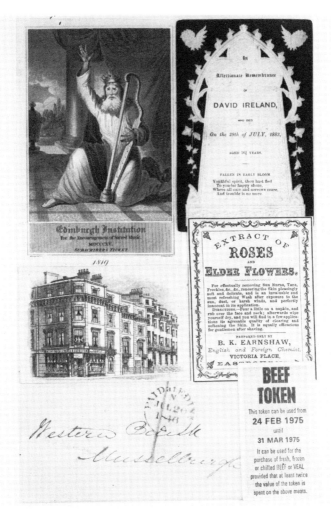

Plate 1

(top left) A subscriber's ticket dated 1819 for the Edinburgh Institution for the Encouragement of Sacred Music founded in 1815. It bears the name of the artist – W. Allan, and of the engraver – A. Wilson.

(top right) An 'In Memoriam' card of 1883 for a boy who died when $16\frac{1}{2}$ years of age.

(centre left) Trade card (*c* 1870) of B. K. Earnshaw, Chemist of Victoria Place, Eastbourne, showing his corner premises in Victoria Place. Note the 'By Appointment' coat-of-arms above the doorway. The reverse side states that the business was established in 1825.

(centre right) A bottle label for Earnshaw's 'Extract of Roses and Elder Flowers'.

(lower left) A letter with a postmark receipt for July 20, 1846 sent by the Western Bank of Scotland at Edinburgh to the Western Bank at Musselburgh. Such letters had no envelope: they were folded and sealed.

(lower right) A recent example of ephemera. Beef tokens were issued to old age pensioners in 1974/75 to enable them to buy beef at a reduced price. How many remain unspent?

Plate 2

(top row) (left) Glass souvenir paperweight with a coloured print of York Minster. *(centre)* Mid-Victorian paper clip in the form of a hand. *(right)* Brass desk-seal with hardwood handle.

(second row) (left) Celluloid paper knife and book-marker with silver mount bearing a registration number for 1893. *(centre)* Penknife with mother-of-pearl handle made at Webster's Sycamore Works. The narrow blades were for cutting quills for pens. *(right)* Edwardian paper knife in the printed advertisement of W. Clarkson of Wardour Street, London, Costumier and Perruquier to His Majesty the King.

(third row) (left) Box of steel gramophone needles with the famous registered trade mark – 'His Master's Voice'. *(left centre)* Carved wooden penholder. *(centre)* Pocket knife with an advertisement for D. & J. McCullum's *Perfection* Scotch Whisky. *(right centre)* Bone penholder and paper knife with a tiny glass insert which when held to the light shows five views of Paris. *(right)* Vesta matchbox of metal covered with tartan cloth.

(fourth row) (left) Box of 'Circular Pointed Pens' by C. Brandauer & Co. These pens neither scratched nor spurted, the points being rounded by a new process. *(right)* Box of pens by William Mitchell.

(below) Sycamore souvenir paper knife by Smiths of Mauchline with a transfer-printed view of 'The Beach, Felixstowe'.

pens in 1858. This almost inspires me to start a collection and this is how many collectors do embark on their hobby – more or less by accident.

The fountain pen which was invented in the 1880s gradually replaced the nib and penholder. The earlier types of vulcanite fountain pens which were filled from a glass fountain-pen filler fitted with a rubber bulb are now true bygones and few lever-fitted pens are still in use. I have just seen a bundle in a bric-a-brac shop at 50p each and no doubt prices will rise. After all, many fountain-pen nibs contain a proportion of gold.

Before the days of fountain pens the traveller had no way of writing in ink unless he carried with him a leak-proof portable inkwell, usually enclosed in a leather case. The pencil therefore was of prime importance, and its point had to be protected. The first propelling pencil which could be carried with ease was invented by Mordan & Hawkins in 1822 and in one form or another the name Mordan was connected with the production of propelling pencils until the outbreak of World War II. Many other firms entered this market and propelling pencils exist in great variety. In some the lead is brought out by sliding a little knob in a slit; in others a knob or cap is turned. All, particularly those of gold or silver and bearing the name of the maker, are sought by collectors. Look out for these four names: S. Mordan & Co, Thornhill, Hicks, and Berry.

Pen Trays

The pen tray is often part of the inkstand, but may be made separately of silver, brass, wood or papier-mâché. They are usually about 25cm long and 6.5cm wide, the metal ones with embossed decoration, others with painted embellishments.

Pounce Pots and Sanders

A knowledgeable collector friend was recently asked to look through the 'rubbish' in a neighbour's garage and found what most people would have assumed to be a rather large pepper-

pot in an old suitcase. He recognised the material as a cream-
ware made by a well-known pottery at Leeds – Hartley,
Greens & Co – which operated from the late 1750s until 1820,
as he had seen similar wares in the Rotherham Museum. It
was, in fact, a pounce pot or sander. Pounce is powdered
pumice, a very fine and gentle abrasive. When the writer of a
letter made a blot or mistake he would erase it and smooth
down the paper by shaking pounce on to the spot, rubbing it
gently with his finger. Similar pots were used for fine sand
which served as blotting paper. The sand was sprinkled on
the damp ink and then shaken off.

Scales
Brass scales for weighing letters and small parcels which were
found on most desks in the nineteenth century, often carry a
small plate attached to the wooden base giving the cost per
ounce of sending a letter. This list can sometimes help to date
the scales. Don't imagine that such scales are of no further use
with the advent of metrication and higher postal charges;
they are now valued as collectors' items.

Seals
From the days of Shakespeare until late Victorian times
important letters were sealed and impressed with the sender's
monogram or heraldic device. This was essential because
until the middle of the nineteenth century letters were not
placed in envelopes; the sheet of writing paper was folded
over and sealed with wax.

Some desk seals are extremely fine but they are rare. The
seal was more commonly kept on the person, often hanging
on a watch chain. Or a seal may have been incorporated in a
ring – the signet ring. Georgian seals are delicate, often with
interlaced metal ribbons used to form the loop for hanging.
Later seals are more massive. Seals are usually made of steel,
glass, marble, or agate set in gold or silver, though occasionally
in brass. Look for the hallmarks (see pp 66–7) which should
tell you if it is gold or silver but remember that not all small

objects carry a hallmark. Do not assume if no hallmark is present that it cannot be a precious metal.

Smoking Accessories

Cigar Cases
In Victorian days, most men who could afford to smoke carried cigars in a special case. There were leather cases, wooden cases transfer-printed with scenes, carved wood cases, and some with a tartan covering. They frequently had divisions inside to prevent the cigars from rubbing against one another. Cases were also made of tortoiseshell, leather, papier-mâché, mother-of-pearl and even japanned metal. They are collected and should be preserved.

Cigar Cutters
Cutters were made for use on a desk or table, to be carried in the pocket, or to hang on a watch chain. The latter were made of gold, silver or nickel and are often very decorative. Cigar cutters were often combined with metal pipe-cleaners.

Cigarette Cases
These were used a good deal when the cheaper cigarettes were packaged in paper and when it was commoner to buy a box of 200 or more, too large for the pocket. Although still used, they are seldom bought second-hand. To have value they must be made of silver or have some special decorative feature. They were also made in elephant or crocodile skin, and some cases of the 1920s have enamelled designs in the *art deco* style. These are sought after.

Cigarette Holders
In the 1920s it was fashionable, especially for ladies, to use very long cigarette holders; some men carried shorter holders. They were often made of the material used for pipe stems – amber, horn or vulcanite – and were carried in velvet-lined cases covered with red leather. Carved meerschaum holders

with amber mouthpieces were sometimes made to resemble a pipe. Early cigarette holders are collected.

Pipes

In the eighteenth century clay pipes were used by all classes and they were used well into the nineteenth century by those who could not afford anything better. This was when the famous 'churchwarden' pipes appeared with very long stems. Clay pipes were brittle and had to be kept carefully in trays or racks. Today, you are much more likely to dig up a clay-pipe bowl or stem in the garden than to find a surviving example indoors.

Two other types of pipe originated in Europe in the eighteenth century. One was made from meerschaum and the other from porcelain. Meerschaum or 'foam of the sea' is a light, porous material which received its name because it was sometimes washed up on the shores of Asia Minor and the Black Sea. It was carved, often in the shape of a human head or grotesque, and then waxed to give it a fine finish. When the pipe was smoked the meerschaum slowly turned a darker colour, first to amber and then to a darker brown. The mouthpiece was usually of amber, wood or ivory and the junction of meerschaum and mouthpiece was usually covered with a silver band. Meerschaum pipes are usually found in velvet-lined cases, often with the name of the retailer.

Porcelain pipes appeared in Germany and Austria at about the same time. They often have painted bowls and are very attractive. However, there was one great disadvantage. Porcelain is not porous and a reservoir had to be fitted beneath the bowl to catch the hot liquid which ran down inside it. This had to be emptied regularly. Meerschaum and porcelain pipes are still made today but few are used in Britain. Victorian examples, however, turn up quite often, usually in a leather case lined with silk.

In the middle of the nineteenth century the hard root of the *bruyère* or tree heath was successfully used for pipes in the Jura Mountains in France, and this material was later exported to many parts of the world. We refer to 'briar' pipes but there is no connection with the English rose briar. Every possible design was used in briar pipes made for the British market and they were often sold in cases. 'Smokers' Companions' were cases with several different briar pipe bowls and stems of amber, horn or vulcanite, providing a range of pipes in one portable pack.

Good early examples of all these types of pipe are now collected, and some collectors widen the field and include pipes from every part of the world. No really old pipe in any material should be thrown away.

Pipe-Stoppers or Tampers
When a smoker lights his pipe he usually presses down the smouldering tobacco with his finger since it tends to rise in the bowl, or he may use the side of a matchbox. From the seventeenth century onwards a special pipe-stopper or tamper was used, although today they are not common. They are small instruments with a circular base to fit the bowl of the pipe. This is attached to a handle two or three inches long. Pipe-stoppers were made in many different materials – close-grained hardwoods, ivory, metal (especially pewter), horn, and even glass and porcelain. The handle is sometimes shaped to represent a well-known historical figure, although common types, made to represent a bottle or barrel, were formerly associated with drinking in taverns. Sometimes the handle unscrews to reveal a miniature corkscrew.

Snuff Boxes
In the eighteenth century tobacco was used in a powdered form and snuff-taking, a habit closely related to smoking, became fashionable. Snuff-taking continued well into the nineteenth century and there are still snuff-takers today. Snuff was carried in small boxes, most of them extremely well made as the lids had to fit tightly so that the fine powder could not escape. Surprisingly large numbers have survived in many materials. Gold and silver boxes were made for those who

could afford them; cheaper boxes were made in brass, pewter, Sheffield plate, and Britannia metal. In Victorian times papier-mâché boxes were produced in large numbers. They had the advantage of being light to carry. Some were just plain black; others were decorated with charming coloured prints of domestic and rural scenes. Horn was also used; the horn was often coloured and was moulded to the desired shape after it had been softened in hot water, although many horn boxes retained the curved shape of the raw material. They were simply fitted with silver lid and mounts. Other materials included mother-of-pearl, shagreen (shark-skin dyed green), and wood.

Wooden snuff boxes are of particular interest. In the middle of the nineteenth century they were sometimes decorated with a wood mosaic veneer and such examples are known as Tunbridge ware. The veneer was prepared by assembling bundles of shaped hardwood sticks of different shapes and colours. These were glued together under pressure and were then sliced across to produce a mosaic veneer which could be glued to the box or other wooden objects as decoration.

Very fine wooden boxes were made even earlier in Scotland with wooden hinges using a process invented by a disabled worker in Perthshire. Many were hand decorated in colour or monochrome with miniature views (plate 4). Wooden snuff boxes with transfer-prints were made by Smiths of Mauchline (see plate 4).

Vesta Boxes
Vesta, the Roman goddess of the earth, gave her name to a new kind of match which became popular soon after Queen Victoria came to the throne. It was tipped with phosphorus and was known as a 'friction light' because it could be readily ignited by rubbing it on a rough surface. For this reason these matches could be dangerous but they were so convenient that they quickly gained popularity. A metal vesta box was made so that they could be carried safely on the person. These usually closed with a spring and had serrations on the base or

side on which a match could be ignited. They were often silver, and were made in large quantities between about 1880 and 1908 when the introduction of the safety match led to an Act of Parliament prohibiting the use of white phosphorus. Vesta boxes were usually gilded inside to prevent corrosion of the silver by the matchheads. Some carried a tiny ring which would be attached to a watch chain or a chatelaine. Silver vesta boxes were often engraved with scrolls, or scenes, or the initials of the owner; some were shaped like books or bottles. They can usually be dated by the hallmarks. Rare and unusual silver vesta boxes have been known to sell for over £40.

Apart from the silver vesta boxes, cheaper matchboxes in brass, tin, wood, ivory, tortoiseshell and other materials were produced in large numbers, some as holiday souvenirs, some to advertise a commercial product – anything from cigarettes to cocoa. They appeared in all sorts of shapes. The example shown (plate 2) of tinned metal with a rectangle of tartan cloth covering the central portion was probably sold as a souvenir in Scotland.

Among the many books on smoking and snuff-taking the following may prove useful:

Dunhill, A. *The Pipe Book* (Barker, 1969)
Hughes, G. B. *English Snuff Boxes* (MacGibbon & Kee, 1971)
Pinto, E. H. and E. R. *Tunbridge and Scottish Souvenir Woodware* (Bell, 1970)
Scott, A. and C. *Tobacco and the Collector* (Parrish, 1966).

Desk Miscellany

All kinds of oddments find their way into the drawers of a desk. Among them:

Coins, Trade Tokens and Commemorative Medals
Old coins or medallions are often found lurking in a drawer

or, much more likely, rattling about in an old tin box. Any keen collector of coins or numismatist views this with great concern for to him the condition of a coin is of paramount importance. Even with modern coins those that have been in circulation or have small scratches or signs of wear on the surface have little interest for him. A worn coin will only attract him if it is a rarity. All coin collectors recognise certain 'states'. These are as follows:

Uncirculated (unc). A term used for a coin straight from the mint or from the headquarters of a bank which has never been used for commercial purposes.

Extremely Fine (EF). A coin that looks as though it may have been uncirculated but does, on close inspection, show small surface marks.

Very Fine (VF). A coin showing a little wear on the raised surfaces.

Fine (F). A coin with considerable wear but not enough to obscure any part of the design.

Georgian and later coins that fall below these standards are normally unacceptable to collectors or are not listed in dealers' catalogues. Seventeenth-century coins are seldom in a state better than 'fine' and for old coins that are extremely rare an even poorer state may be acceptable.

Faced with a box of coins, therefore, the first job is to pick out those which are 'fine' or better and to make sure that they are kept in separate envelopes so that they do not rub against one another. If they are British coins it should be possible to get some idea of their value by consulting *Seaby's Standard Catalogue of Coins of England and the United Kingdom* or *The Coin Year Book* published annually by the Numismatic Publishing Company. Remember that the dealer's buying price may be only about half to two-thirds of the catalogue value since he has to maintain his premises and make a profit. He will be very critical indeed of condition since he knows that he can sell an 'extremely fine' coin for as much as six times the selling price of a 'fine' one, and he may not wish to buy relatively common coins which he already has in stock.

There will be a temptation to clean coins before trying to sell them. On no account do so. Preparations sold for cleaning silver, copper and brass may contain abrasives and cause further wear. The tarnishing or 'patina' on coins is expected and adds rather than detracts from their value. So simply wash coins in soapy water to remove any greasy film.

It is possible that you may find a sovereign case with old coins. These cases date from Victorian and Edwardian times when sovereigns were in common use. They are small circular cases which were carried on watch chains. Inside there is a sprung plate which is pressed down when a sovereign is inserted. They normally held five or six coins. Some were combined with vesta boxes.

You may also come across what appears at first sight to be a coin but when examined more closely is seen to carry the name of an inn or a trader of some kind. These are trade tokens which may be made of a baser metal such as tin or lead. They were issued in many localities when there were not enough official coins to go round as small change. Thousands were issued in the seventeenth century during the Commonwealth period and the reign of Charles II, and at the end of the eighteenth century there was another major issue around 1787. They were nearly all of small denominations – pennies, half-pennies and farthings. More details may be found in the following:

Seaby, P. and Bussell, M. (Editors) *British Tokens and Their Values* (Seaby, 1970)
Whiting, J. R. S. *Trade Tokens* (David & Charles, 1971).

Commemorative medals are sometimes found among collections of coins. These have been struck since the sixteenth century to mark important events. In the nineteenth century, especially after the Great Exhibition of 1851, they appeared in considerable numbers. Whenever Queen Victoria opened a new building or a park it provided an occasion for striking a medal. These commemoratives which have an historic interest are collected. Don't throw them away: find out more about them in one of the following:

> Edmundson, J. *Collecting Modern Commemorative Medals* (Pelham Books, 1972)
> Whiting, J. R. S. *Commemorative Medals* (David & Charles, 1972).

If you have a collection of coins or individual coins you believe to be valuable take them to your nearest coin dealer. You will find coin dealers listed in the yellow pages of the telephone book. Alternatively, consult a good auctioneer; many hold special coin sales. If you live near London you can go to one of the coins specialists such as B. A. Seaby of Audley House, Margaret Street, W1 (the firm which issues the annual coin catalogue) or Spinks of Duke Street, St James's, SW1. Regular auction sales of coins are held by Glendennings of Blenheim Street, W1 and Sotheby's of Bond Street W1A 2AA.

Military Relics

Men and women who have spent part of their lives in the armed services often keep mementoes of the period. Such relics are generally grouped under the title of militaria and there are many dealers who specialise in this field.

Metal buttons and badges from service uniforms are keenly sought by collectors and their value depends mainly on age and rarity. They may well be found in one of the tin boxes in which cigarettes or chocolate were sent to the troops with a message from the reigning sovereign at the time. These have value, particularly the boxes sent by Queen Victoria during the Boer War.

Medals may also be found in a desk drawer. These are usually still attached to their ribbons. Medals were awarded for gallantry, to those who took part in particular campaigns, and to all those who took part in a particular war. War medals are, of course, very common but campaign and gallantry medals are rarer. For example, only 579 Victoria Crosses were awarded in the four years of World War I. Such medals have a particular interest because it is usually possible to trace the story attached to them – the identity of the recipient, the action concerned, and where, when and under what circumstances he displayed the gallantry that led to the award. If you come across old medals it is well worth consulting a specialist dealer but before doing so try to gather all the information you can about them. Books to consult on small militaria are:

Hall, D. and Wingate, C. *British Orders, Decorations and Medals* (Balfour Publications, 1973)

Joslin, E. C. *The Standard Catalogue of Orders, Decorations and Medals* (Spink & Son Ltd, 1972)

Purvis, A. A. *Collecting Medals and Decorations* (Seaby, 1971)

Squire, G. *Buttons* (Muller, 1972).

Costume and Needlework

In the nineteenth century dress was regarded as having great importance. The Paris fashions of the period were carefully studied in the magazines whose editors arranged for coloured fashion plates to be sent from Paris to be bound in with an English text. Some have survived in such publications as *The Englishwoman's Domestic Magazine* which used plates by the best-known French fashion plate artist – Jules David. These hand coloured engravings are of great interest to all who study fashion and are often framed to provide attractive wall decoration.

Very occasionally early costumes have survived in old trunks or chests. Even if they have suffered damage from moth and decay they should be carefully preserved together with any of the accompanying fashion accessories. Fans, for example, provide superb examples of craftsmanship in ivory, carved wood or lace. Some were made with painted parchment or ostrich feathers.

Fans will always sell at auction but there is not such a demand for early costumes, although there is a Costume Society which aims to promote the preservation of significant examples. The best course of action if you wish to ensure that a good costume is preserved is to consult the curator of the nearest museum. Many museums display costumes and there are several museums devoted entirely to early costume – at Bath, Bexhill-on-Sea, Manchester (Platt Hall), and Rugeley (Blithfield Hall), for example.

A number of small accessories are valued by collectors. These include:

Buttons and Button hooks
The buttons used in the eighteenth and nineteenth centuries were often of great beauty and may occasionally be found

in the odd box which has been kept for many years in case they might one day 'come in useful'. Old buttons are, of course, much more desirable if they are in sets. Apart from the fact that they can sometimes be used, they are greatly prized by collectors, especially in America. Look particularly for hand-chased gilts, gold-plated sporting buttons with little hunting scenes, French enamel buttons, hand-painted porcelain buttons, Chinese ivories and silk-on-wood buttons. Even those made of jet which were widely used by the Victorians, especially during periods of mourning, have their interest. Many fine silver buttons, often with enamel decoration showing the heads of young ladies with long flowing hair, were made during the art nouveau period (from about 1885 to World War I). In the days when servants wore livery, special livery buttons were made with family crests. All these are collected. See:

Peacock, P. *Buttons for the Collector* (David & Charles, 1972).

Small buttons were used on boots and to fasten the long gloves which often reached to the elbow. For this reason the button hook was in general use over a long period, certainly from 1860 to 1914. They were used to draw the small circular buttons through the button holes. The hooked end was pushed through the button hole, manoeuvred round the button shank, and a quick pull and twist then secured the button. The smaller button hooks, used for gloves, were often made of silver and a hallmark, if present, will enable you to date it. Many were fashioned to be carried in a bag or purse, and close like a penknife. Cheaper ones of steel were made to fold up (plate 3).

The larger button hooks used to fasten boots, had to be stronger and are usually steel with handles of bone, ivory or mother-of-pearl. Some button hooks had a little ring attached to the end of the handle so that they could be hung from a chatelaine. Chatelaines were clasps which could be fastened to a lady's waist with a chain or chains from which small objects

31

could be hung ready for immediate use. They were used for keys, pencils, notebooks, seals, watches, vesta boxes and leather-covered purses.

Buckles

Buckles are sometimes found in the button-box. Today they are used to fasten belts but in the eighteenth century they were used on shoes before laces became popular. The commoner buckles were of steel or brass but many were edged with silver. The steel functional parts have often rusted over but it is worth working on a good old silver buckle to try to bring it back as nearly as possible to its original condition. Some Dutch silver buckles have intricate moulded designs. There is always a ready market for silver buckles since there is a tradition among nurses that they should wear a silver buckle on their uniform belts when they qualify.

Card Cases

In Victorian times it was customary in polite society for a lady to leave a visiting card when making a social call. These were carried in card cases. Early examples were made in silver with a slip-off lid but later all kinds of decorative cases were produced. They include mother-of-pearl cases with hinged lids, and cases of carved ivory, black lacquer, carved or transfer-printed wood, painted papier-mâché, tortoiseshell and Tunbridge ware.

Chain Purses

Small purses of foreign manufacture of nickel or silver chain mesh were often made with a ring so that they could be hung from a chatelaine. They were common in late Victorian and Edwardian times and some were even made of gold.

Hatpins

Ladies' hats became very large at the turn of the century and had to be anchored in some way, normally to the hair by means of a hatpin. These were usually four or five inches long but very long ones were used in Edwardian days. The head of the pin which showed outside the hat had to look decorative and great ingenuity went into the design of this. Pinheads were made of silver, brass, enamel, tortoiseshell, ivory, mother-of-pearl, shells, coloured stones and many other materials. Many were button-shaped or spherical. Brass regimental or livery buttons were sometimes used for the purpose. Occasionally a lady might cover the pinhead with material to make it suitable for a mourning outfit.

Hatpins were often placed in a stand of some kind on the dressing table. The pottery example in the shape of a bull (plate 8) with holes pierced in his back for the pins is unusual. Some hatpin holders were very like pen holders; others like sugar casters but without a hole in the base.

Hatpins provide an attractive field for the collector of modest means so don't throw them away, particularly if you find them in the box in which they were originally sold.

Lockets

Lockets are small hinged ornaments which were worn, particularly in late Victorian times, to remind the owner of a 'loved one far away' or of a 'dear departed'. They were made of silver, brass or other metal, often in the shape of a heart, and they were fitted with a hinge so that a lock of hair or a very small photograph could be kept inside beneath glass. They were often hung from a necklace.

Embroidery, Lace and Patchwork

Embroidery

From the beginning of Queen Victoria's reign until about 1875 embroidery was synonymous with Berlin woolwork. The idea of drawing designs on squared paper and indicating the colours to be used for each part of the pattern originated in Germany in 1801. In due course these designs were printed and hand-coloured so that they could be sold for copying on to a square-mesh canvas. By 1840 some 14,000 designs were available and many were imported into Britain by a Regent Street dealer. The embroidery was done with soft wools and became a craze: practically every household took it up making upholstery for chairs and sofas, for foot-stools and music-stools. It was used for the panels of firescreens, for cushions and tea-cosies. Every type of design was produced – flowers, exotic birds, baskets of fruit and religious scenes. Many of the scenes were based on well-known paintings or engravings, especially those with animals. Landseer's work was a prime source. These were mounted on panels and framed for wall decoration. However, after about 1860, the ideas of John Ruskin and William Morris began to have some influence and designs began to include ornamental scrolls and geometrical motifs. Colours were less strident and the work altogether more delicate.

Beadwork developed from Berlin woolwork. Beads were sometimes worked into designs to provide highlights and eventually coloured beads replaced the woollen stitches altogether on many small objects such as pincushions, purses (plate 3), tea cosies and slippers. So-called miser's or stocking purses were usually made of fine mesh or beadwork. They were used by men as well as women. The coins were inserted through a slit and were kept in place by a sliding metal ring. Victorian woolwork or beadwork is of no great value but will always sell at auction as embroidery of the period.

By 1875 the influence of the Arts and Crafts Movement had transformed the art of embroidery. A Royal School of Art Needlework had been founded with over 100 embroiderers who spread a new gospel – that really old needlework of earlier centuries should be studied and with the lessons learned the embroiderers should use original designs or patterns drawn by skilled artists. Much late Victorian embroidery of this period is crewel work which involved the use of thin worsteds. It derived from Jacobean embroidery and one of the favourite designs was the 'Tree of Life', long winding stems with stylised foliage, used particularly on linen and cotton twill bed hangings and curtains.

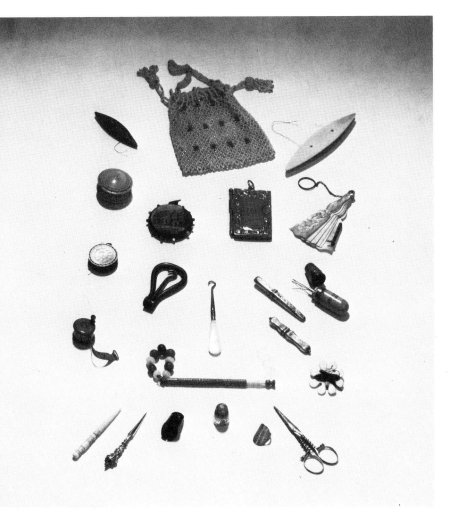

Plate 3

(top row) (left) Wooden tatting shuttle. *(centre)* Beadwork purse. *(right)* Ivory tatting shuttle.

(second row) (left) Three circular pin cushions of ivory, mother-of-pearl and glass (with coloured print of Lady Godiva and Peeping Tom). *(centre)* A paper note pad with hinged metal covers and pencil and *(right)* an ivory-leaf note case in mother-of-pearl covers with pencil. Both are equipped with rings so that they may be hung on a chatelaine.

(third row) (left) Tape measure in wooden case with winder. *(centre)* Buttonhooks, one of steel for boots with hinge to fold it; the other with mother-of-pearl handle for gloves. *(right)* Three needle holders: two silver and one with an advertisement.

(fourth row) (centre) Wooden lace bobbin weighted with coloured beads. *(right)* Ivory holder for odd pieces of thread.

(fifth row) (left) Two stilettos, one of ivory, the other of metal. *(centre)* A silver thimble and two nail protectors, one of tortoiseshell, the other of ridged metal. *(right)* Pair of sewing scissors decorated with snake motifs.

Plate 4

(top row) (left) Wooden box with sliding lid on which there is a contemporary print of 'A View of Both Houses of Parliament on the Night of the 16 October, 1834'. An ink signature of the owner on the underside of the lid is dated 1841. There are several inkstained compartments inside suggesting that it may have at some time been used on a desk for seals and other writing equipment. *(centre)* Ivory box with screw top probably used as a pin box. *(right)* Souvenir box of sycamore wood by the Smiths of Mauchline, Scotland with a black transfer-printed view of Carisbrooke Castle.

(second row) (left) Tunbridge ware snuff box with pull-off cover. *(centre)* Hand-decorated wooden snuff box with a Laurencekirk wooden hinge. Snuff boxes of this type were made at several localities in Scotland in the first half of the nineteenth century. *(right)* Cardboard box covered with pink silk brocade and small sea shells.

(third row) (left) Piqué snuff box of tortoiseshell inlaid with gold. *(right)* Snuff box with lid and base of bevelled agate panels set in engine-turned metal.

Silks were used for many of the more delicate designs and in these a Japanese influence can be recognised. All late Victorian embroidery tends to be in softer colours, especially browns and greens, than the earlier Berlin woolwork. If you find any fine pieces of embroidery which would appear to be of Victorian origin some care should be taken to see that they are well presented, especially if they are to be sold at auction; otherwise they may be jumbled up with other textiles and escape attention. Place each piece of embroidery on a piece of stiff card (unless it is too large) and enclose it in a transparent plastic bag, telling the auctioneer what you believe it to be. In this way the viewer's attention will be attracted.

Lace

In Victorian and Edwardian times lace was used on clothing as well as for decoration on handkerchiefs, tablecloths and napkins. A few years ago boxes of old lace fetched very little. Today the situation has changed and people are beginning to regard lace as a beautiful antique.

Much early lace was hand-made and traditional methods of lace making continued in certain parts of the country well into the present century, in the Honiton area of South Devon, for example. Some lace was made using a needle and is known as needlepoint lace; some on a pillow using bobbins. The pattern was marked out on the 'pillow' with pins and the lace was made by twisting the many threads together. Each thread was attached to the top of a bobbin which hung down over the side of the pillow. The bobbin shank was held between thumb and finger and, in order to make sure that it would fall back into place when released, it was weighted with a circlet of glass beads which were coloured to enable the lace maker to identify the threads. These bobbins are now collectors' items. They were mostly made of wood, bone or ivory and were sometimes decorated with bands of pewter or some other metal. They were often given as love tokens. Particularly sought after are examples with a girl's name or sentimental message etched upon them.

C

A good deal of nineteenth-century lace has survived since it took up little room and was often stored flat in a cardboard box in a drawer. In sorting through old lace there may be pieces that you find puzzling. A few definitions may help:

A *Bertha*, or berthe, was the name given to the deep falling collar encircling the neck on a low-necked dress. When spread out on a flat surface it forms a complete circle.

Fichu was the name for a small triangular lace shawl for the shoulders and neck.

Flounces were strips of lace sewn to the skirt of a dress; they were sold as either 'Court Flounces' or 'Bridal Flounces'.

Lappets were lace flaps for a head-dress.

Plastron was the ornamental front on a bodice.

Tippets were worn on the shoulders of a dress and had long ends which hung down the front.

A *Tucker* was a 'modesty' piece of lace worn with a low-necked dress.

The identification of the various types of old lace and the probable country of origin is a job for the specialist. It should be possible, however, even for the uninitiated to distinguish hand-made lace from the lace made by machine, and to judge whether it has age and quality, and therefore value. Don't worry too much if the lace you find in a drawer is discoloured, or even a little torn. It is often not as fragile as it looks and will usually wash well if treated with care. Restoration is another matter. It needs considerable skill and the fine linen thread needed for repair work will have to be taken from another piece of old lace.

Patchwork

'Waste not want not' was an important adage for the poorer Victorian housewife. When she had made dresses and curtains she used up the surplus pieces of cloth by sewing them together to make patchwork. In those days of large families

Shuttles

Shuttles were used for 'tatting', a knotted lace edging made by hand from sewing thread. They are elliptical in shape with pointed ends and when made of ivory are often finely engraved.

Silk Winders

These are flat and shaped like a flower with five petals. They were used for storing odd lengths of embroidery silk (plate 3).

Stilettos

Small, round, dagger-like instruments, usually of bone or ivory, were used before the days of stainless steel, for unpicking stitches or for pricking out a pattern (plate 3). For this purpose a piece of paper with the drawn design was placed over the material, the outline was pricked to make a series of small holes in the paper and then chalk powder was sprinkled over the holes and rubbed in with a pad. When the paper was removed the pattern was outlined in chalk on the material.

Tape Measures

These were often called 'yard measures' and were wound on a spindle within a bone, ivory or wooden box (plate 3).

Thimbles

Thimbles are the most highly prized of all needlework accessories largely because a collection can be attractively displayed and because they are found in many materials. They were widely used before the advent of the sewing machine and were often very decorative. Although most thimbles are made of silver or some other metal they can also be found in mother-of-pearl, porcelain, ivory, enamel, wood and glass. The silver thimbles are often chased with attractive designs and may sometimes be inset with pearls or coral. Many were kept in thimble cases. Look carefully for a hallmark on a silver thimble which will enable you to date it. There may also be a very small inscription indicating that it was made to commemorate a coronation or jubilee. Some carry the name of the owner. Nail protectors were made of metal or tortoise-shell to slip on to a finger liable to be pricked by an embroidery needle (plate 3).

Thread Holders
These were essentially for silk or cotton thread. If you come across examples that are barrel-shaped with a small hole in the side, and are fitted with a spindle and a tiny handle, they are almost certainly Georgian or early Victorian holders used before thread was sold on a wooden reel.

Thread Waxers
It was customary in Victorian times to wax threads, partly to strengthen them and partly to make them easier to use. The wax was sold in a little cake wrapped in paper and the thread was pulled across it.

Work Companions
Small portable cases known as 'work companions' were made with a limited number of accessories, usually scissors, stiletto, needlecase, bodkin, crochet hook and thimble. Almost any combination could be made up to suit the individual customer. This made it possible for a lady to continue her needlework when away from home. See:

Andere, M. *Old Needlework Boxes and Tools* (David & Charles, 1971)
Groves, S. *The History of Needlework Tools and Accessories* (David & Charles, 1973).

Games and Toys

Games and toys change with the years; those that are popular today are very different from those of the nineteenth century although certain types have persisted over long periods.

Card Games
It is not uncommon to come across a pack of cards that was printed 50 or more years ago, although the older a pack is, the less likely it is to be complete. The first task is therefore to check that there are, in fact, 52 cards in the pack. How can one distinguish an old pack from a modern one? There was a duty on playing cards from the eighteenth century until 1960 when it was abolished. In the early days the amount was stated on the rather elaborate ace of spades. In 1862 it was stabilised at three pence and the amount was stated on the wrapper though many packs of cards still kept an elaborate ace of spades. The originator of the modern playing card was Thomas de la Rue who first printed cards with a high gloss in the reign of William IV. At that time cards were produced to be viewed one way with the kings, queens and knaves as three-quarter-length figures. They became double-ended in 1862 though patience cards were still printed with full-length court cards up to 1890. The printing of A, K, Q and J on the ace and court cards and of figures on the cards of lower value came later. The reverse side of a playing card sometimes gives a clue which helps to date it. Many carry old advertisements (plate 6) and I have a 'Coronation' pack in which each card bears a portrait of Edward VIII, printed to mark an event which never took place. Packs much sought after are those with an American 'Jeep' on the back printed in Belgium in 1944 in the expectation of an Allied victory. See:

Beal, G. *Playing Cards and Their Story* (David & Charles, 1975)

Tilley, R. *The History of Playing Cards* (Studio Vista, 1973).

All kinds of games were played with cards especially children's games. 'Happy Families' and 'Snap' are perhaps the best known. I recently found a set of 'Snap' cards among a lot of old toys (see plate 6). These were designed by John Tenniel (1820–1914), who also designed a set for 'Happy Families'. He was a cartoonist for *Punch* from 1850 to 1901 and illustrated books, including *Alice in Wonderland* (1865). The set was in the original packet with the name of the maker – John Jacques & Son of 102 Hatton Garden, London, a firm which published many card games for children.

Mother-of-pearl counters were used for scoring in card games from the beginning of the eighteenth century and these often took the form of a small fish engraved with a decorative design. Cribbage games are scored on a board with rows of small holes into which pegs are inserted. Old boards are often finely inlaid. Take care to preserve the original pegs.

Chess and Chessmen
Chess was a popular game in the fifteenth century and has had its addicts ever since. The 32 chessmen vary greatly in form. Usually they are of wood but some are most beautifully carved in ivory or jade and a complete set in these materials can be very valuable. Chessmen were also made in pottery by such firms as Doulton and Wedgwood.

Good chessmen should be preserved even if a set is incomplete. Odd pieces sometimes sell quite well to a dealer who can use them to complete a set. Collectors of chessmen, as distinct from players of chess, often restrict themselves to single pieces, partly to save expense but also to display them effectively without overcrowding.

Fine chess boxes which open out to form a chess board of inlaid wood are much sought after.

Dinky Toys
Clockwork trains and constructional meccano were invented

by Frank Hornby before World War I. Similar trains were made by Marklin, B/Lowke and other firms in Germany. Miniature motor vehicles appeared in the 1920s but the Dinky toys issued by Meccano Ltd in 1934 are perhaps the best known. The models produced before the outbreak of war in 1939 were extremely well made and are sought after for their rarity. However, despite the fact that standards have fallen, any Dinky toy made before 1965 can be regarded as a collector's item. They are not easy to date without reference to an early catalogue or advertisements in old issues of the *Meccano Magazine*, particularly as many early models were re-issued after the war. Look to see if the tyres are made of smooth white rubber and show signs of having been silver coated. Look underneath: a yellowish paint was used before the war and a black paint afterwards. It may be possible to borrow a copy of Cecil Gibson's *History of British Dinky Toys 1934–1964* (Mikansue, 1973). This lists nearly a thousand different models made over a thirty-year period and has some useful illustrations. There are, of course, several other makes of miniature vehicles – Corgi, Yesteryear, Matchbox etc. All are collected. Don't throw away damaged examples. They can often be restored, or they may have value for their spare parts. Some idea of the enormous variety of miniatures available to the collector can be gained by studying the part-collection of toy cars and lorries shown on plate 5. The full collection of 26,000 models amassed since 1956 is estimated to be worth over £20,000.

Dolls and Dolls' Houses

Late Victorian and Edwardian dolls are those most likely to be found today, although not always in their original state. They may be wax dolls or bisque dolls. Wax dolls were made by making a shell of a type of papier-mâché and coating it with wax, the hair being held in a slit in the head. The bodies were stuffed with sawdust or straw. Most wax dolls were made in England. The most famous maker was Madame Montanari of Fitzroy Square, London, but, as few wax dolls carry a mark, it is seldom possible to attribute a doll to a particular maker.

Most bisque dolls were made in Germany. 'Bisque' is an unglazed porcelain used to make the heads. These are connected by elastic to the body and legs of the dolls which are of a composition material. The maker's name is usually found to be impressed on the back of the head. Noted makers include Simon and Halbig, Schoenau and Hoffmeister, Cuno and Otto Dressel, and Armand Marseille.

If you find an old doll in poor condition, on no account throw it away. Perfectly good dolls can be assembled from parts. I have seen a box of doll fragments – heads, bodies, arms and legs sell for over £20. Complete old dolls in good condition fetch a good deal more.

Miniature pieces of furniture, china and glass – in fact any household miniatures which can furnish a dolls' house – are in very great demand. Insignificant though they may seem to be they often fetch high prices. See:

Desmonde, K. *Dolls and Dolls' Houses* (Charles Letts, 1972).

Jigsaw Puzzles
Jigsaw puzzles have been made for over two hundred years. The earliest were intended as teaching aids for children. They were made by mounting a hand-coloured map on a thin piece of wood which was cut along the country or county boundary lines. Well-known nineteenth-century makers included Betts, Darton, Spooner and Barfoot. Look out for the first three names. The Barfoot family used a spray of pink roses as a trade mark. However, really old puzzles are not common but any puzzle dating from before about 1930 can be regarded as a collector's piece. In many cases the subject matter helps to date a puzzle but make sure it is complete before offering it for sale.

Model Soldiers
In late Victorian times model soldiers were made of lead or

a lead alloy and this material was used until it was largely replaced by plastic in the 1960s. The lead was painted over with the colours of the uniforms used in every war – the Cuban War, Omdurman, the Boer War and right up to World War II, covering all the opposing troops. France and Germany dominated the market in the early days: the two leading firms were Mignot & Lucotte and Heinrichsen & Heyde. Models were produced in large quantities and sold in labelled boxes. The German ones were made of solid lead.

In 1893 a British firm, appropriately called William Britain, began to make hollow-cast models which could be sold more cheaply and they soon captured much of the market. Other makers included Courtenay, Greenwood, Hunt, and Ping & Stadden. Lead soldiers often turn up among old toys, though seldom in their original boxes.

A friend of mine recently unearthed a small suitcase full of lead soldiers, some in their original boxes, and they made a splendid array when set out on a table. They were sent to a saleroom and fetched several hundred pounds. A few damaged ones were later sold to a dealer who restores lead soldiers. Most auctioneers will include model soldiers in their sales. Phillips of Blenheim Street, London, hold four specialist sales of lead soldiers every year. It is an advantage if you can describe them accurately when entering them for a sale. The following books will help:

Garratt, J. G. *Collecting Model Soldiers* (David & Charles, 1974)

Richards, L. W. *Old British Model Soldiers 1893–1915* (Arms and Armour Press, 1970)

Taylor, A. *Discovering Model Soldiers* (Shire Publications, 1972).

Picture Blocks and Building Blocks
Picture blocks consisted of cubes of wood, either stencilled with the letters of the alphabet or covered with squares of coloured paper which could be arranged to form a picture.

47

They were intended to be educational. The building blocks intended solely for constructional play probably came later. These included other shapes in addition to the cube. You may come across building blocks of red and white stone. These were made in Edwardian times by the German firm of Richter but they had the disadvantage of being extremely heavy.

There are many other toys that can be found in old toy cupboards including all kinds of wooden puzzles, spinning tops, hoops and so on. Before you throw away old toys try to arrange to visit one of the museums of childhood which include:

The Museum of Childhood and Costume at Blithfield Hall, near Rugeley, Staffordshire; the Playthings Past Museum, Beaconwood, Beacon Lane, near Bromsgrove; The Museum of Childhood, 38 High Street, Edinburgh; The National Toy Collection now housed at The Grange, Rottingdean, Brighton; and The Doll Museum, Oken's House, Castle Street, Warwick.

Over 80 other museums which exhibit children's dolls and toys are listed in *Museums and Galleries in Great Britain and Ireland* published annually by ABC Historic Publications, Oldhill, London Road, Dunstable, Bedfordshire.

Scrapbooks and Albums

In the nineteenth century there was a craze for keeping albums, which lasted until about 1914. Even between the wars people continued to keep albums of photographs, postcards, cigarette cards and, of course, stamps which are probably more widely collected today than ever before.

Autograph Albums
You may well come across an album with pastel-coloured paper which was once carried round to cricket matches, concerts and theatres in the hope that the owner might acquire the signature of some well-known player, musician, actor or actress. Although relatively few of these books are now of any great interest, I have seen one such album, beautifully kept, with the signatures of many musicians accompanied by their photographs, which were acquired from various sources. Not long ago I bought an old autograph album in a bric-a-brac shop for 15p. Stuck lightly to one of the pages was a letter from H. G. Wells written from Dunmow in Essex to a friend who had sent him a book. Letters are of much more interest than a mere signature for they usually reveal something of the personality of the writer. So look carefully at autograph books before throwing them out to see if they contain any autographs or writings of well-known people. Some people collect such autographs, among them R. Rawlins who has written a comprehensive book on the subject – *Four Hundred Years of British Autographs* (Dent, 1970).

Cigarette Card Albums
The first cards to be inserted in cigarette packets were merely cardboard stiffeners to prevent cigarettes from being crushed in their rather flimsy paper packs. In America the stiffener soon carried printed material: the earliest in 1880 was used for election propaganda. By 1891 a number of firms were

producing printed cards, usually with advertising material, though one American firm had already produced some 40 or more pictorial sets of cards with special albums for collectors. Britain was not far behind. The early sets printed during the reign of Queen Victoria are now worth a good deal of money and in clean condition are very rare. Apart from Wills and Players, which have issued a great many series over the years, the following firms were publishing cigarette cards in the 1890s – Adkins (soldiers); Conden's (beauty spots); Faulkner's (puzzle cards); Ogden's (who were the first to use the photographic form and issued series of lady cricketers and footballers); Salmon & Gluckstein (heroes of the Transvaal); South Wales Tobacco Co (views of London); T. E. Yeoman's (beautiful women). Few of these sets turn up today but Edwardian and later cards are often found among the possessions of people whose childhood was spent before 1940. By the outbreak of World War I it is estimated that some 2,500 series had been issued.

After 1914 printed silks often took the place of printed cards in the larger packets of cigarettes. They were issued by such firms as BDV, Kensitas, and Singleton & Cole Ltd. National flags and regimental badges were favourite subjects. They were very attractive and I have seen them framed, a dozen at a time, for wall decoration.

If you want to dispose of old cigarette cards it is worth consulting a copy of *Exchange and Mart* in which many dealers advertise for them. You may, however, find it useful before accepting an offer to consult one of the catalogues advertised by the larger dealers, which can be bought for about £1. Some auction rooms sell cigarette cards; consult your local auctioneer. See:

Genders, R. *Guide to Collecting Trade and Cigarette Cards* (Pelham Books, 1975).

Family Crest Albums
At one time it was customary for titled people to use writing

paper carrying their embossed family crest in colour. These crests were often cut out by the recipients of their letters and mounted in a crest album sold for the purpose. These are still of interest to students of heraldry and have some value despite the fact that this form of collecting has virtually ceased. Such albums should be offered to a secondhand book dealer or entered in a sale of books or antiques.

Matchbox Labels

Old matchbox labels are usually mounted by collectors in an album and the hobby is still very much alive today. These pictorial labels were first stuck on boxes of 'lucifers' as they were then known in the 1830s. The practice spread all over the world. The field is therefore enormous. Individual labels, particularly the modern British varieties, are worth very little but there are plenty of old labels from other countries that will sell for over £1 each. If you find an old fusee box, don't remove the label. It will sell well as it stands, particularly if complete with contents.

The *Exchange and Mart* carries advertisements for match-box labels and often advertises booklets which will give further information. See:

Rendell, J. *Matchbox Labels* (David & Charles, 1968).

Photograph Albums

Photography started in the second quarter of the nineteenth century and any examples which can be dated to within this period are of particular interest. The daguerreotype, named after the Frenchman, Jacques Mandé Daguerre, may well turn up in an old box or drawer. For many years portraits were taken by the process he invented. They are usually 5cm × 8cm, or sometimes 7cm × 8cm, though larger ones were taken. The photographs would have a very delicate surface which had to be protected from the air by covering with glass. Daguerreotypes are therefore in cases, usually with a gilt mount which prevents the protective glass from touching the surface, or occasionally examples are found in a frame. Later photographs were treated in the same way but a daguerreo-type can readily be identified since it has a highly reflective surface and must be held at an angle if the image is to be seen clearly. Good daguerreotypes now fetch several pounds and may be even more valuable if the portrait is of a well-known person and the name and address of the photographer is on the case.

In the 1850s a new 'wet plate collodion' process became popular. This was simpler than the earlier experimental processes and the numbers of professional portrait photographers started to increase rapidly. They produced photographs in two main sizes – the 'cabinet' size, roughly 14cm × 10cm and the 'carte-de-visite' size 9.5cm × 5.5cm, so-called because they frequently were used as visiting cards. The photographs were sold mounted on stiff board which acted as the trade card of the photographer. In late Victorian times with further technical advances the stream became a torrent and by the turn of the century there were 17,000 registered professional photographers, mainly taking portraits. Almost every family had a photograph album bound in embossed leather and fitted with a brass clasp; the pages were often colour-printed with decorative flowers.

These old albums can be of great interest to the collector, particularly if they contain very early photographs of unusual subjects. They are also significant to people who study the costume and social habits of the nineteenth century.

Albums can readily be sold, particularly if they are in good condition and individual cabinet and carte-de-visite photographs are often offered for sale in book and bric-a-brac shops. The two examples in plate 6 have a period significance as they reflect the costumes and furnishings of the day.

Some albums open to reveal a space at the back where some of the pages have been replaced by a small musical box which will play several tunes. If in good condition these sell very well indeed.

Stereoscope photography gave rise to the production of prints mounted in pairs on cards. Each photograph was of the

Plate 5

Part of a collection of 26,000 models amassed by a York collector of Dinky and other toy cars and lorries. The complete collection is estimated to be worth well over £20,000. (*Associated Newspapers*)

Plate 6

(top left) A card from the Victorian game of 'Snap'. The design by John Tenniel, illustrator of Lewis Carroll's *Alice in Wonderland* (1865) and *Through the Looking Glass* (1872).

(top right) Playing card from an Andrews Liver Salt pack issued in the late 1940s for free distribution to trade customers.

(lower left) Photograph of a Victorian gentleman seated in a button-back chair at a Davenport and holding a quill pen, dated 1865. This was taken by John Burton & Sons who were the sole photographers for the Tercentenary Shakespeare Festival at Stratford-upon-Avon in 1864. This is stated on the mount which forms the trade card. It shows the Royal coat-of-arms and indicates that John Burton & Sons who had studios in Leicester, Derby, Birmingham, Nottingham and Burton-on-Trent were patronised by HM The Queen, HRH The Prince of Wales and HRH The Princess of Wales.

(lower right) Photograph of three young ladies in typical Victorian costume taken by E. Watson of Peebles. The trade card mount was designed and printed by Spicer Brothers of London.

same subject taken from a slightly different angle. When these were viewed through a stereoscope with two lenses the viewer saw a picture with a third dimension. The most popular stereoscope was one which could be held in the hand. Stereoscopes and stereo-cards are now in demand again on both sides of the Atlantic. If you cannot find a dealer in old photographs who will take them, try entering them in an auction sale.

Postcard Albums
Between about 1895 and the 1920s the postcard album was almost as important as the family photograph album. Although pictorial postcards had been used in several European countries prior to 1890 the first picture postcard was not made available in Britain until 1894 and then had to conform to certain standards. The first cards had to be printed so that only a name and address appeared on the stamp side. As a result the picture on the other side was printed so that a wide margin was left for the sender to use for his message. It was not until 1902 that the stamp side was divided so that the left-hand side could be used for a message. From this time the picture occupied the whole of one side of the card.

Postcards were carefully treasured in albums – both unused cards bought as mementoes of a holiday or visit and cards sent by friends and relatives. Today there are hundreds of specialist collectors of postcards and an album full of early cards can fetch a considerable sum of money though few collectors concern themselves with cards printed after about 1930. Used cards can often be roughly dated by the postmark, or if this is undecipherable, the stamp will at least indicate the reigning sovereign when it was sent. In general, of course, the older the card the more interest it is likely to hold for the collector. There are specialist collectors of postcards of actors and actresses, disasters, exhibitions, motor cars, ships, railway engines, aircraft, royal portraits, sporting scenes and wartime scenes. Humorous cards are immensely popular, especially those by such artists as Bruce Bairnsfather, Tom Brown,

Donald McGill, Phil May, W. Heath Robinson and Louis Wain.

During World War I many greetings cards were embroidered in coloured silks by French or Belgian women with appropriate messages for the British troops to send home. Some had a small pocket with a little card for a personal message. These are also very popular with collectors.

Many dealers advertise for postcards and some of them are to be found at the London Postcard Centre, 21 Kensington Park Road, London W11, where it is possible to discuss prices with dealers and to negotiate on the spot. However, you can assess roughly what the *retail selling value* of cards may be by studying the *IPM Catalogue of Picture Postcards* issued by the Internation Postcard Market Ltd, 96 Idmiston Road, West Norwood, London SE27 9HL. General information about postcards is given in:

Alderson, F. *The Comic Postcard in English Life* (David & Charles, 1970)
Carline, R. *Pictures in the Post* (Gordon Fraser, 1971)
Holt, T. & V. *Picture Postcards of the Golden Age* (Mac-Gibbon & Kee, 1971)
Klamkin, M. *Picture Postcards* (David & Charles, 1974).

Scrapbooks

It was the custom for a young person to collect together all kinds of decorative pieces of paper including advertisements cut from magazines, pictures from newspapers and journals, greetings cards of all kinds, especially Christmas cards and Valentines, and the coloured sticky scraps which could be bought from the local stationer. These were arranged on the pages of a scrapbook to suit the taste or whim of the owner; the result was very personal. Some even include poems in copper-plate writing, occasionally original but more usually copied from a book of poems, often with pencil, pen or water-colour drawings to illustrate them. Some are superbly planned with great artistry; others are rough and ready. These scrap

56

albums are now valued as reflections of the life and attitudes of the period. A good scrap album should be left intact though some specialist collectors of early Christmas cards, for example, may be tempted to try to remove these for their collections. A good scrap album will always sell well.

Stamp Albums

Old stamp collections are often unearthed when a clearance is made. They are worth looking at carefully as any stamp dealer will tell you. It may take a good deal of time but it is well worth sitting down with an up-to-date catalogue in an attempt to make a rough valuation. If you do this, ignore all stamps with a catalogue value of less than 10p – these will be common and of relatively little interest to a dealer who will, however, be interested in stamps worth £1 or more *provided they are in good condition.* Having made a rough valuation, re-check the highest values you have noted. It is very easy to jump to the conclusion that a stamp is worth about £30 without making sure that the one you have is exactly the same as that listed in the catalogue with the right perforations, watermark, colour etc. If your rough valuation of a collection comes to £40, for example, do not assume that you will sell it for that price. You will be fortunate to get as much as one-third or one half of your valuation. It depends a good deal on the demand for the particular stamps you have. British and Commonwealth stamps rate high, as do American stamps; on the other hand it may be difficult to dispose of those from South America or the Near East. Be sure to make an allowance for condition. Even an unused stamp has already lost some value if it has been stuck down with a stamp hinge in an album. As with coins, don't let good stamps jostle together in a cardboard box. Place them carefully in a stock book, or temporarily between the pages of any book.

Stamps can, of course, be sold at auction but this can be a tricky business. The large London auction rooms are primarily interested in really valuable stamps, often individual stamps, though there are some provincial salerooms which hold stamp auctions. A run-of-the-mill collection should probably be offered to a dealer who is looking for opportunities to acquire stock.

Stamped envelopes or 'covers' are very often found with a stamp collection. Try to decide why these have been kept in their arrival state. They may be first-day covers which are widely collected or they may have been kept because they have interesting postmarks. Postmarks are attractive to collectors if they are of some unusual place, or were franked at an exhibition or other event. Postmarks such as TPO (Travelling Post Office), RSO (Railway Sub-Office), Field Post Office or Army Post Office are all sought after.

Sorting Through Books

Nothing harms a book more rapidly than allowing it to get damp or dropping it on the ground. Mould forms on the covers of a damp book and small brown spots form on the surface of certain types of paper, a state known as 'foxing'. A dropped book will have bumped corners and a weak spine. So if you have to sort through books treat them with care and respect. If you cannot do the job at once see that they are stacked carefully in a really dry and well-ventilated room. A month or so in a damp place may take pounds off their value.

Sorting through books to separate the valuable from the ordinary, and the ordinary from the valueless is a job for a specialist but a few hints may be useful for those who want to make at least a preliminary assessment themselves.

Antiquarian Books
This is not an easy term to define but for practical purposes one may assume that an antiquarian book is any book over a hundred years old. Such books will normally be bound in leather, half-leather, or in a slightly ridged cloth which may have a distinctive style of embossed or gilded decoration typical of Victorian bindings. Fortunately most antiquarian books carry a date on the title page. Many antiquarian books, even novels, were published in three volumes. So the first thing is to discover if you have a single *complete* book or several volumes which can be assembled to create a single work. Odd volumes are usually of very little value.

Many books have engravings, plates or folding maps. Sometimes a plate may have been removed, or a map may have become detached. Go through the book to make sure that every page is intact and that no plates or engravings have been removed. The fact that plates are missing will reduce the value of a book but it is not necessarily worthless for this reason. Books of engravings can still be valuable for the illustrations that remain even if many are missing or some have become detached. Such books are known as 'breakers' because they are usually broken up for the plates.

Valuable books usually pass through one of the main auction rooms and their prices are recorded in an annual publication known as *Book Auction Records* which can be found in many public libraries. The books are listed under authors and sometimes several editions of a particular book are listed. If a book you have is listed note the price it fetched at auction but don't immediately assume that your copy will reach the same figure. Much depends on the condition of a book, the edition and so on.

Some people tend to brush aside what to them appear to be 'dull' books yet these may well be books wanted by academic libraries in this country or abroad. It is true, however, that many religious books are in little demand even if they are over two hundred years old unless there is some particularly interesting feature to recommend them.

First Editions

Most collectors like to assemble first editions of the books written by an author in whom they are particularly interested. This applies not only to antiquarian books but to books published in this century. They should be preserved, preferably in the original binding and dust jacket.

When sorting books you can therefore reject most reprints and book club editions as 'reading copies': they have relatively little value. How does one recognise a first edition? It is much easier to recognise what is not a first edition. Most publishers when reprinting a book that has sold well will make this clear on the reverse of the title page. Some publishers merely give a date on the title page and this may suggest that the book is a first edition. This is by no means always so. It is necessary to check against a bibliography or other reference book to make sure that this was, in fact, the date of the very first publication. Most good booksellers have access to detailed bibliographies and will be able to advise you if you wish to sell a particular book. However, there are several books which are useful for quick reference. *Everyman's Dictionary of Literary Biography* which offers a concise account of the most notable British and American authors, gives the dates of publication of many of their best-known works. Legouis and Cazamian's *History of English Literature* has long and detailed footnotes listing the first publication dates of books by notable authors. Both these books are published by Dent and are kept up-to-date.

Children's Books
Special books for children have been produced since the seventeenth century. Early examples are rare. One is more likely to come across nineteenth-century children's books most of which are highly moral tales or books of instruction, especially those designed to help children learn the alphabet. In Victorian times, with the advent of colour-printing, children's books multiplied and a number of first-class artists were commissioned as designers and illustrators. Look out for books illustrated by the following: Randolph Caldecott (1846–86), Walter Crane (1845–1915), Kate Greenaway (1846–1901), Beatrix Potter (1866–1943), Arthur Rackham (1867–1937), Edmund Dulac (1882–1953).

Well produced books with colour illustrations by any of these artists can be of considerable value if they are first or limited editions in good condition.

Stories written for girls and boys in late Victorian and Edwardian times were usually bound in pictorial covers. The earlier examples had cloth covers with impressed designs in gilt, later books had the pictures printed on cloth in full colour. School stories and adventure stories were extremely popular and were produced in large numbers. Many authors were incredibly prolific. First editions of these stories are now in considerable demand.

The authors of stories for boys include R. M. Ballantyne, Captain Brereton, Harry Collingwood, G. Manville Fenn, G. A. Henty, W. H. G. Kingston, Talbot Baines Reed, Captain

Mayne Reid, Herbert Strang and Percy F. Westerman. Their works are fully described in Eric Quayle's *The Collector's Book of Boys' Stories* (Studio Vista, 1973).

Stories for girls were written by Helen Bannerman, Angela Brazil, Edith Nesbit, Gene Stratton-Porter, Bertha Upton and Florence Upton (who invented the 'golliwog'). It is by no means easy to decide whether any one of their books is a first edition or not: many issues do not even bear a date. *Who's Who of Children's Literature*, edited by B. Doyle (Hugh Evelyn, 1968) is a useful reference book on juvenile literature.

Illustrated Books

Many books are now valued as much, or more, for the work of their illustrators as for that of their authors. If you are sorting through books look particularly for the following names: Cecil Aldin (1870–1935), Edward Ardizzone (1900–), George Armour (1864–1949), Aubrey Beardsley (1872–98), Thomas Bewick (1753–1828), George Cruickshank (1792–1878), Gustav Doré (1833–83), Richard Doyle (1824–83), Joan Hassall (1906–), Jessie M. King (1876–1948), Edward Lear (1812–88), Clare Leighton (1899–), Mervyn Peake (1911–68), W. Heath Robinson (1874–1944), Sir John Tenniel (1820–1914), Hugh Thomson (1860–1920), Louis Wain (1860–1939), and Rex Whistler (1905–44).

First editions and limited editions of books illustrated by all the above artists are keenly sought by collectors and in many cases later editions are also in demand. The condition of such illustrated books is, of course, of great importance.

Specialist Subjects

Many antiquarian and out-of-print books are sought by specialist booksellers. Topographical books on a particular area will sell better to a second-hand bookseller in that area than to one remote from it unless he happens to specialise in topography. If you come across a whole shelf of books on a single subject it is well worthwhile seeking out the particular bookseller likely to be interested.

A list of specialists with names and addresses of their premises is given in the *Annual Directory of Booksellers in the British Isles Specialising in Antiquarian and Out-of-Print Books* published by The Clique Ltd, 75 World's End Road, Handsworth Wood, Birmingham B20 2NS.

Maps

Old Ordnance Survey maps are sought by local historians who study the changing face of Britain. Indeed, the first and early editions are now hard to find. So, if you come across any old maps, especially any issued before World War I, in plain printed covers, don't throw them away. If you want to know more about their interest and value consult *The Historian's Guide to Ordnance Survey Maps* published by the National Council of Social Service, 26 Bedford Square, London WC1.

Newspapers and Journals

Occasionally in an attic or cupboard a few really old papers may be found which have been kept for some specific reason or just overlooked. There are many collectors of historic newspapers and students of press history who look for particularly interesting issues. Newspapers reporting such events as the sinking of the *Titanic* or the dropping of the first atom bomb, victory days of the major wars and royal events are particularly desirable.

Pause before you throw away old magazines, particularly long runs of literary publications. *The Strand Magazines*, for example, of 1891–3 published Arthur Conan Doyle's *Adventures of Sherlock Holmes* and these issues are sought by all collectors of his first editions. The following often contain similar 'firsts' or articles by eminent authors – *The Adelphi, Arena, Argosy, Atalanta, The Bell, The Bibelot, Blackwood's Magazine, The Book Collector, The Cornhill Magazine, Encounter, The English Review, The Fortnightly Review, Irish Writing, The London Magazine, The London Mercury, The Nineteenth Century, The Pall Mall Magazine,*

Penguin New Writing, Picture Post, The Poetry Review, The Transatlantic Review, and *The Weekend Review.*

Reputable art magazines such as *Apollo, The Connoisseur* and *The Studio* also have a market among antique dealers and collectors as reference material.

Great interest has been shown recently in children's comic papers. These were a Victorian innovation. They were first launched in their present form in 1874 with a paper called *Funny Folks.* Then followed *Comic Cuts, Funny Cuts, The Big Budget* and *Ally Sloper's Half Holiday.* Not surprisingly, very few have survived though just occasionally a bundle turns up in an attic. However, comics published before the end of World War I and even later may be of considerable value. A run of *The Butterfly* from 1906 to 1939 recently made £450 at auction and a run of *Film Fun* from 1920 to 1942 fetched the same figure. A five year run of *The Mickey Mouse Weekly* (1936–41) made £500. Look out for *The Bull's Eye, Hotspur, The Magnet, The Rover* and the *Wild West Weekly* and preserve them carefully.

Bookplates

Inside the front cover of some books you will find the book-plate of an owner: a rectangular piece of paper with a printed coat-of-arms, crest, or special design usually with the owner's name, the whole symbolic of his ancestry or his interests. In many cases it is sacrilege to remove this from the book, for it is interesting to know that a well-known politician read the works of Bernard Shaw or that a famous or eminent scientist owned books by Joseph Conrad and Rudyard Kipling. However, not all bookplates are those of notabilities, nor are all books with bookplates notable books. So if some books are to be discarded either because they are already falling to pieces or because they have little value as books, save the bookplates.

Ephemera in Books

Before you dispose of any books go through the pages for ephemera. You will be surprised to find that readers have used all manner of things as bookmarks – old postcards, envelopes, photographs, tickets and, of course, bookmarks printed for the purpose. Hundreds of different bookmarkers have been issued in the past century by firms advertising their products, by insurance companies, publishers, booksellers, charitable organisations, government departments, and local libraries. For several years I carefully kept all the bookmarkers I found in old books until I had formed a considerable collection, part of which is described in *Collecting Bookmarkers* (David & Charles, 1974).

Finally, a word about dust jackets. Some people discard these before putting the books they have acquired on their shelves, but many have been designed by first-class artists. Several of the illustrators mentioned on page 62 have also designed dust jackets and you will find that many of the artists are given a credit on the flap of the dust wrapper, or have signed their work. Look particularly for wrappers by Michael Ayrton, Edward Bawden, Cecil Beaton, B. S. Biro, John Farleigh, Philip Gough, Felix Kelly, Lynton Lamb, Osbert Lancaster, Charles Mozley, John Nash, John Piper and Rex Whistler among others. I have saved many fine dust wrappers from oblivion in recent years. They are now mounted and filed and I look through them frequently: they form my private gallery of modern commercial art.

A Word about Metals

Silver

It is important to be able to distinguish between silver and silver-plated goods. Never assume that an article is not made of silver because of its general appearance. Examine it very carefully to see if there is a hallmark of any kind. This mark is made by an assay office where every piece of silver must, by law, be tested. Four or five marks are usually punched on the silver when it has been tested. They include:

1. The Assay Mark made to show that the piece has at least 92·5 per cent of the pure metal. This mark is a guarantee that the piece is of sterling quality. On English silver the mark is a Lion Passant. This is the stamp of a lion walking with one forepaw raised and it has been used without a break since 1719. In Edinburgh a thistle has been used since 1759 and in Glasgow a Lion Rampant, with both forepaws raised, has been used since 1819. The Dublin assay mark shows Hibernia seated with a harp.

2. The Hallmark – which gives its name to the four or five marks together – indicates where a piece has been assayed. It is the mark of origin. There are now assay offices in Birmingham, Dublin, Edinburgh, Sheffield and London. The marks of origin are respectively an anchor, a crowned harp, a castle, a crown and a leopard's head.

3. The Date Letter records the year when the piece was assayed. It consists of a single letter of the alphabet in a particular style of print and shape of shield. These vary with each assay office and are listed in the many books of hallmarks.

4. The Sovereign's Head appears on silver assayed between 1784 and 1890 to indicate that the duty levied on silver during this period had been duly paid.

5. The Maker's Mark which usually consists of the initials of the silversmith who made the piece.

Imported foreign silver has to pass through an assay office to be marked before it can be sold as Sterling Silver. If it reaches this standard it will be punched with the mark of the importer, an assay mark, a decimal figure indicating its quality and the usual annual date letter. The assay marks for foreign silver are the sign of Leo in London, an equilateral triangle in Birmingham, the sign of Libra in Sheffield and St Andrew's Cross in Edinburgh.

Much silver-plated ware bears a mark similar to a hallmark. The only way to be sure that a piece is made of silver is to find the assay mark. If it is not present the article is unlikely to be silver. There are exceptions. Very small decorative pieces, for example, are occasionally not hallmarked if it is considered that the mark would destroy their artistic appearance. One would expect a small silver thimble, however, to bear a hallmark. Note that every part of a piece assembled from separate parts should bear a hallmark. A lidded coffee-pot, for example, should have a hallmark on the pot itself and another on the lid even though the two parts are joined by a hinge. The marks should be identical.

If a piece has been polished so much that the hallmark can no longer be deciphered it has lost a good deal of its original value.

If you have silver to dispose of it is worth acquiring the latest edition of a very inexpensive and useful pocket book of marks – F. Bradbury's *Guide to Marks of Origin on British and Irish Silver* published by J. W. Northend Ltd, of West Street, Sheffield S1 3SH. Don't hesitate to have good silver professionally valued before selling. Even small pieces may be worth far more than you may imagine, particularly if they are of early silver and have been made by a noted silversmith.

Sheffield Plate

An important discovery was made in the 1740s making it

possible to produce an article that looked like silver but could be produced much more cheaply. It happened in Sheffield when a cutler was repairing the handle of a knife. While doing this he touched some copper with heated silver and the two metals fused together so that they could be hammered or rolled as though they were one. He was soon fusing thin sheets of silver to either side of thicker sheets of copper and making boxes and thimbles from the fused metals so that only the silver layers showed. This came to be known as Sheffield Plate and it opened up a vast new market. Nearly everything that had been made of silver could satisfactorily be made of the new Sheffield Plate. Most early plate of this kind bears the name and symbol of the maker. These are listed in M. M. Macdonald-Taylor's *Dictionary of Marks* published by *The Connoisseur*. However, not all Sheffield Plate is marked. It is usually possible to identify old examples as much wear will have removed the thin silver layer in places to reveal the copper-coloured metal beneath. Look particularly at edges and corners for this 'bleeding'.

Britannia Metal

This new material was patented in 1842 and was exhibited by James Dixon and Sons of Sheffield at the Great Exhibition of 1851. It is a rather soft alloy of tin, antimony and copper. When new and well polished it looks very much like silver but with age acquires a dull patina. There was a large export of Britannia Metal to America in the nineteenth century where it is now collected. Although not particularly attractive, pieces in good condition do still have a market value.

Electro-Plated Wares

The discovery that a thin layer of silver could be deposited on a base metal or alloy by electrolysis opened up another new field. The object was made first from the alloy and plated afterwards. The method was developed at the Elkington factory in Birmingham and was used by other firms under licence. By 1860 it had superseded all other methods of plating

68

because of its convenience and cheapness. The plating was mainly done on nickel silver (such pieces usually bear the letters EPNS), and occasionally on German silver. This had the advantage over Sheffield Plate that, when the surface layer began to wear, the metal beneath was much the same colour. Moreover, worn articles could be replated to restore them to their original brilliance. See:

Wardle, P. *Victorian Silver and Silver Plate* (Herbert Jenkins, 1963).

Pewter

Pewter was for centuries the poor man's silver, particularly for household utensils – chargers, plates, mugs, measures etc. Today old pewter has a high value. It is usually an alloy of tin and lead, though some types include antimony, bismuth or copper. When new it looks rather like dull silver but with time the surface gradually oxidises, producing a typical grey patina which becomes harder and deeper with age. Good early pewter usually has 'touch marks', the equivalent of the hallmark on silver but larger. These are the maker's marks registered with the Pewterer's Company. The standard quality pewter was stamped with a Tudor rose, pieces of higher quality with an X. Pewter mugs continued to be made throughout the nineteenth century for use in inns and taverns. After 1824 it became obligatory to stamp all such drinking vessels with their capacity and the initials of the reigning sovereign. It is possible therefore to find GR, WR, and VR on nineteenth-century tankards. From 1877 a crown was added to the VR which makes it easy to recognise a late piece.

If you come across old pewter, treat it carefully, it is a very malleable metal and if dented is stretched. On no account try to clean and polish pewter because this detracts from its value. You will be destroying a patina that it may have taken over two hundred years to acquire. See:

Jackson, R. *English Pewter Touch Marks* (W. Foulsham, 1970).

Gold and Pinchbeck

Gold jewellery should always be marked with its carat value. From 1854 five standards were recognised – 22, 18, 15, 12 and 9 carats – these are the standards of purity: pure gold is 24 carats. In 1932 a new standard of 14 carats replaced the 15 and 12 carat standards. If you can find no marks on a piece that appears to be gold it may be made of pinchbeck. Christopher Pinchbeck, a London clockmaker in the seventeenth century, discovered that by mixing zinc and copper in certain proportions he could produce an alloy that would polish and, when gilded, look very like pure gold. It could also be chased or embossed like gold and even when the gilding became worn the metal showing beneath was of the same colour. Pinchbeck was widely used in Victorian jewellery.

Brass and Copper

It is now fairly well known that objects made of brass or copper often have considerable value, especially genuine old horse brasses and decorative fireside furniture – trivets, fenders, fire-irons and coal scuttles. Don't throw away the brass handles, lock plates, hinges and castors from old furniture that has disintegrated: these can be used to advantage by the furniture restorer.

You may not immediately recognise old copper or brass as such if it has been stored away for some time in a loft, garden shed or garage. A small wooden box with metal bands rescued from the dirt and dust of an old shed recently sold for £3. The wood proved to be mahogany and the metal bands were brass. When both were cleaned and polished the box fetched £30 in an auction sale.

Bronze

Bronze is usually described as an alloy of copper and tin but other metals such as zinc, lead or nickel are often added in smaller proportion. It has been used for centuries for casting sculpture. It is heavy and takes on a fine, smooth patina. Bronze sculpture is valuable and the models of animals made

Plate 7

(top left) A postcard of the 1920s when 'wireless' sets with headphones were rapidly gaining in popularity. This is No. 5095 of the 'Comique' series issued by Inter-Art Co of Florence House, Barnes, London SW.

(top right) An Edwardian card in the 'Summer' series issued by Bamforth & Co Ltd of Holmfirth, Yorkshire, one of the most prolific producers of comic postcards.

(lower left) A World War I card by Donald McGill, perhaps the most famous of all comic postcard artists. Issued by Inter-Art Co as No 2386 of their 'Comique Series'.

(lower right) A postcard issued shortly before World War I ridiculing the idea of Women's Suffrage. The postmark is dated '1 Sept 1914'. The work of women during the war changed public opinion in their favour. This card was printed in Germany for a series issued by 'B.B. London'.

Plate 8

(top row) (left) A gophering iron. *(centre)* Victorian glass wasp or fly trap. *(right)* Pottery hat-pin holder in the shape of a bull made in Portugal.
(second row) (left) A flat-iron with the cast mark of D. Nash, Smethwick. *(centre)* Pierced iron-stand of handworked brass. *(right)* A fairing showing a married couple with twins in a cot between them. It is inscribed 'Looking down upon his luck'. The base bears a circular mark – 'Made in Germany'.
(third row) (left) A pottery pap boat made by Minton of Stoke-on-Trent. *(centre)* A porcelain model of Shakespeare's House by W. H. Goss with his Goshawk printed mark and a registration number for 1894. *(right)* A pottery feeding bottle transfer-printed with a floral design.
(fourth row) (left) Pot lid transfer-printed in black with the words 'Cold Cream' within a decorative border. *(centre)* Colour-printed tin made for Cadbury Bros of Bourneville by Hudson Scott & Sons Ltd of Carlisle to commemorate the 'Coronation of King Edward VII and Queen Alexandra 20th June 1902'. *(right)* Pair of blue and white transfer-printed knife rests made in Staffordshire for John Mortlock of London in the 1820s. They bear an impressed Mortlock mark.
(below) Ebony glove stretchers with spring hinge.

by the French sculptors of the nineteenth century known as 'The Animaliers' are widely collected. However, do not assume that you have found a bronze sculpture when you unearth a decorative ornament in the shape of a statuette, a prancing horse or hunting dogs. It is far more likely to be made of spelter, a lighter base metal made to imitate bronze. Ormolu is gilded bronze and has been used for mounts on fine furniture and for clock cases. Gilded spelter has also been used for clock cases. If in doubt about the difference between bronze and spelter ask a good clockmaker or an auctioneer to advise you.

Bronze was also used by bell-founders who nearly always cast their initials on the inside of their bells, even on small bells for farmers to use on their horses and other stock, and on hand bells. Look for the initials RW which stand for Robert Wells, a famous eighteenth-century bellmaker of Aldbourne in Wiltshire. W & RC stand for William and Robert Cor of the same village; and JB for James Burrough of Devizes.

Iron

Cast iron was widely used by the Victorians for grates, doorporters, footscrapers and many other practical purposes. These are described in more detail in the chapter on 'Bygones' (pp 93–102).

Electrical and Mechanical Bygones

Cameras

Many people are fascinated by the history of photography and several major auction rooms hold sales of 'photographiana' – mainly old photographs and photographic equipment including cameras, enlargers, stereoscopes etc. Any early wooden dry-plate camera dating from the 1880s is now regarded as a vintage camera. So are early Kodak cameras and the first Brownie box cameras which were launched on the market in 1900. Later cameras also appear in sales. In fact any camera made before World War II has some historic value and will probably command a higher price than many later examples which are merely regarded by the photographer of today as 'out-of-date'.

Folding pocket Kodaks made before 1914 which had a wooden front standard have fetched well over £50 and even the Vest Pocket Kodak (VPK), which George Eastman gave to members of the American Expeditionary Force who served in France in World War I, now has a commercial value. Early Newman & Guardia cameras such as their reflex and their *Trellis* camera (1910–1930) are sought after. So is the *Duchessa*, a small plate camera of the 1920s and the *Pilot*, a twin lens reflex of the 1930s. Do not assume, therefore, that an old camera is worthless: it is probably appreciating in value day by day. See:

Smith, R. C. *Antique Cameras* (David & Charles, 1975).

Clocks and Watches

Many old clocks and watches, which have ceased to function, are often thought by their owners to be not worth repairing. This may well be true of some late Victorian and Edwardian clocks that were mass-produced in America, Britain and Germany. However, there are many clock-enthusiasts who get great pleasure just from making an old clock work again. I have never seen one of these old clocks fail to sell in an auction room.

Much the same is true of watches. Indeed, the silver watches which Edwardian gentlemen carried on a chain in their waist-coat pockets sell extremely well.

Gramophones and Phonographs

The first attempt to record sound that could be 'played back' was made by Thomas Edison who, in 1877, succeeded by cutting an imprint on a cylindrical drum covered in tinfoil. This led in due course to the 'Edison Home Phonograph'. A more permanent recording was later made on wax as a result of further experiments by A. G. and C. Bell. These early phonographs, which continued to be made well into the twentieth century, are now collectors' pieces. An Edison Bell 'Domestic A' gramophone made by Pathé Frères just after the turn of the century recently fetched £160 at auction.

The first attempt to record sound on flat discs made of glass was made by Emile Berliner, a German emigrant to the USA. By 1888 he had perfected a method of duplicating his recordings from a master copy. The recordings were made by the direct action of sound waves on a diaphragm. In the 1920s electrical recording and electrical reproduction became possible with a standard speed of 78 revolutions per minute. Thirty years later the long playing record with a speed of $33\frac{1}{3}$ revolutions per minute began to establish itself and earlier gramophones and records were gradually made obsolete. Nevertheless, if you find any old machines or records don't throw them away. They may be valuable. Even the boxes of steel needles used with early machines should be preserved.

The pre-World War I gramophones sold to the public normally had a cabinet with a double- or triple-spring motor which could be wound while playing, a tapered arm attachment to hold a steel needle, a 10 inch or 12 inch turntable, a sound box and a 'Morning Glory' horn. Two of the best-known examples were the 'Melba' and the 'Monarch'. If you think you have a gramophone of this period try to consult the booklet on *Talking Machines* issued by the Science Museum in London.

Records were made of singers, instrumental soloists and bands: in fact, of the kind of music that might have been played in the best hotels and in popular concert halls. Recordings of the most famous artists such as Enrico Caruso, Madame Melba and Adelina Patti cost rather more than those by other artists.

The Columbia and HMV machines usually fetch the best prices today but almost any type will reach double figures including the Algraphone, Cliftophone, Perophone, Seymour, Vesper and Vocalian.

Knife Cleaners and Marmalade Cutters

Before the days of stainless steel ordinary table knives rusted very quickly. They had constantly to be cleaned and many large households had a machine to do the job. Knife cleaning machines consisted of a circular wooden box mounted on a stand with holes in the circumference of the box into which the knives could be inserted. They were cleaned by turning a handle at the side.

Another machine used in the Victorian kitchen was the marmalade cutter. A machine by Follons and Bate Ltd, patent of Manchester, was recently offered for £4.

Any old kitchen equipment of the period is now worth money – including old metal coffee grinders.

Magic Lanterns and Moving Pictures

The first magic lantern was a simple device for projecting a still picture on to a screen. It consisted of a tin box fitted with a chimney, a lens holder, and a slide used to push the pictures into place. The source of illumination was an ordinary candle or nightlight. The slides themselves were usually long and narrow with several pictures painted in colour on the glass. The operator slid these through the lantern showing one picture at a time. Later on, refinements were added. These were telescopic front tubes to hold the lenses, and the necessary adaptations to make it possible to illuminate with paraffin, acetylene or gas. Any piece of apparatus of this type, and any early slides should be retained for sale to collectors.

Model Engines

Before World War I toys were being made to 'embody the principles of mechanics' including simple cranes, drawbridges, swing bridges and cable railways. The mechanical toys of most interest to the collector, however, are those which were made to operate by steam.

Model steam locomotives with spirit burners were made in Germany and sold commercially from about 1870 together with rails, passenger cars, trucks, vans etc. These models were all very finely made and can be restored by a good mechanic if they are damaged. Still more desirable are some of the engines built to scale by amateurs.

Musical Boxes

All kinds of devices have been used to produce music mechanically but the cylinder musical box is the one most likely to be found in an attic or box room for they were made in large numbers so that families could have music in their homes without having to make it themselves. Cylinder musical boxes were made from about 1820 until World War I. They have wooden cases, often beautifully veneered or inlaid with brass or mother-of-pearl because they were articles of furniture emitting sounds and therefore the centre of attention. However, after about 1875 they were made in such large numbers that cheaper boxes became the norm. Since the industry evolved from the watch craft in Switzerland, which flourished in the eighteenth century, it is not surprising to find that most musical boxes are Swiss-made. Geneva and St Croix were the major centres though boxes were also made in Paris, Berlin, Prague and New York. Many makers' names are found on boxes, and some stamped their names on the movements. You may find names such as Alibert of Paris; Bremond, Langdorff, Lecoultre or Nicole Frères of Geneva; or Marmod Frères of St Croix. If there is no name there may be a trade mark. A very full list of makers and agents is given in Graham Webb's *The Cylinder Musical Box Handbook* (Faber & Faber, 1968) which deals mainly with the restoration of old musical boxes.

The polyphon musical box, which largely superseded the cylindrical musical box, had perforated steel discs and was usually sold with 12 tunes. It played automatically and was made with an 'elegant walnut case'.

Sewing Machines

The first practical sewing machine was made by the American inventor, Isaac Merritt Singer, in 1857 and within two years the Singer Manufacturing Company was in production in New York. The early Singer machine was sometimes known as 'The Grasshopper'. A Boston firm, Grover & Baker, was also making a sewing machine in the 1860s and the firm of Wilcox & Gibbs was early in the field. In Germany, an early machine was made by Junker & Ruh of Karlsruhe, Bavaria. Other names to look out for are Fisher & Gibbons, Wheeler & Wilson, and Moldacot – a pocket machine which could be clamped on to a table. The first electric machine appeared in 1889. If you have a Victorian machine you wish to dispose of, try putting it in an auction sale. See:

Jewell, Brian. *Veteran Sewing Machines: A Collector's Guide* (David & Charles, 1975).

Telephone Instruments

Old telephone instruments are in demand not only by collectors but also as theatrical 'props'. The 'candlestick' type should sell for over £5 and the old wall boxes of the 1880s for a good deal more.

Typewriters

Various 'writing machines' were invented and patented in the eighteenth century but the earliest typewriter to be produced commercially was the Scholes & Glidden machine which appeared in the 1870s and was made by the Remington firm of New Jersey, USA. It was a clumsy-looking affair on a metal stand. Other machines began to appear in the next twenty years and these typewriters dating back to Victoria's reign still turn up from time to time in attics and cupboards. Some are thrown away; others find their way into private collections or museums via the auction rooms. The British Typewriter Museum at 137 Stewart Road, Bournemouth, is well worth a visit.

Old machines to look out for are the Blickenderfer, New Century Calligraph, Columbia, Desmore, Empire, Hammond, Hartford, Invincible, Jewitt, Keyston, Lambert & Blick, Maskelyn, Merritt, Oliver, Portal, Royal Barlock Salter, Smith Premier, Sun, Swift, Williams and Yost. Clearly there was an enormous market for typewriters even before World War I. Some were sold in oak or walnut cases. If you have one and want to sell it, try an advertisement.

Vacuum Cleaners
The early vacuum cleaners were very large machines and few have survived. One of the earliest was a 'Baby Daisy' machine, now a museum piece.

Wireless Sets
Early wireless sets are attracting more and more interest. Crystal sets which were produced before about 1925 needed no batteries but the listener did require earphones. By 1925 valve sets with loud-speakers had been introduced and there were many enthusiasts who bought components and built their own sets. Commercial sets were often made of bakelite. If you find any early wireless equipment don't throw it away even if you can't get a sound from it.

Further information about some of the mechanical bygones mentioned in this chapter can be found in:

Pearsall, R. *Collecting Mechanical Antiques* (David & Charles, 1973).

Old Glass and China

The range of articles made of china and glass is enormous, particularly if 'china' is taken to include pottery as it is when we speak of a 'china shop'. It is important to be able to decide whether a piece of china is old or relatively modern and there are some clues which will help.

Fortunately, many pieces of pottery and porcelain bear marks, usually on the base. These often help with information about makers and dates. Always look carefully at these marks. The following notes will help you to interpret them:

1. If the word ENGLAND appears in the mark you may assume that the piece was made *after* 1891. If MADE IN ENGLAND appears then the piece was made this century.

2. Although bone china was first made early in the nineteenth century the words BONE CHINA were not used in marks before about 1900.

3. The words TRADE MARK were introduced by the Trade Marks Registration Act of 1875.

4. If you see an actual date on a piece of pottery or porcelain it is almost certainly intended to indicate the date of establishment of the firm that made it. Wares made by the firm of Thomas Wood & Sons sometimes bear eighteenth-century dates since the family have been potters for over two hundred years.

5. Some pieces bear a diamond-shaped registration mark. This was introduced in 1842 when it became possible to register a design with the Patent Office. The class of goods is indicated by a number in roman numerals at the top, in this case IV stands for china and glass. The figure F is the one that concerns us because this indicates the year of registration. (The D, left, states the month, the 4, right, the day of the month, and the 10 is a parcel number.)

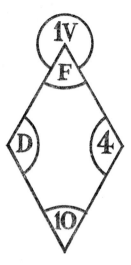

The letters of the alphabet did not run consecutively so that the following key is needed:

A = 1845	J	= 1854	S	= 1849
B = 1858	K	= 1857	T	= 1867
C = 1844	L	= 1856	U	= 1848
D = 1852	M	= 1859	V	= 1850
E = 1855	N	= 1864	W	= 1865
F = 1847	O	= 1862	X	= 1842
G = 1863	P	= 1851	Y	= 1853
H = 1843	Q	= 1866	Z	= 1860
I = 1846	R	= 1861		

When the letters of the alphabet had been used the place of the year number was changed. From 1868 it appeared on the right of the diamond and the dates ran:

A = 1871	I	= 1872	U	= 1874
C = 1870	J	= 1880	V	= 1876
D = 1878	K	= 1883	W	= 1878
E = 1881	L	= 1882	X	= 1868
F = 1873	P	= 1877	Y	= 1879
H = 1869	S	= 1875		

In 1884 this system was abandoned in favour of numbers which ran consecutively. Within a year numbers had reached five figures. Rd No 29784, for example was registered in 1885. In 1889 the numbers reached six figures. Rd No 200,000 was registered in 1892; Rd No 300,000 in 1897; Rd No 400,000 in 1902 and Rd No 500,000 in 1907.

Registration marks are therefore invaluable in helping to date pieces of any kind. However, do not assume that any particular article was actually made in the year of registration. The designs were protected for three years, and designs could be re-registered. It is possible to say, however, that goods bearing a registration mark were probably made within a year or so after registration.

Bottles

Glass bottles have already attracted the attention of collectors who now go digging in old Victorian rubbish heaps to unearth out-of-date varieties. So many have now come on the market that the prices have dropped but, nevertheless, really interesting old bottles of glass or stoneware will still fetch a pound or so.

So don't throw away any really old bottles during a house clearance. They are fairly easy to recognise; the glass is often a pale blue or greenish colour and contains many small bubbles. The rim of the neck will be irregular: indeed, the makers seldom formed a rim on old ink bottles. The neck was left rough. Mineral water bottles were often moulded with the name of the firm that finally sold them. The examples with a neck containing a glass marble stopper have a ready market.

Children's Plates

Early in the nineteenth century the custom was established of giving children special plates for their food, and this spread throughout the country in Victoria's reign. Some had the alphabet impressed or printed on the rim; many were printed with nursery rhymes or proverbs with entertaining pictures of

82

flowers or birds, or with pictures of characters from children's books such as *Robinson Crusoe*. They were made in Swansea, Staffordshire and on Tyneside and Wearside in the North East. These plates were produced in enormous variety though relatively few have survived. If you find one, treasure it or sell it (for quite a good sum) to someone who will.

Decorative Plaques and Plates

There have always been people who have liked to hang plates on the wall instead of pictures. Some may be of little value; others may now have some age and be worth a considerable amount. If you have any to sell be very careful when you try to remove the wire hangers which may well have rusted. It is very easy to chip a plate unless this is done with care.

Some time ago I saw two decorative Imari plates sell for 40p at a stall in aid of charity. A month later I saw the same two plates sell in the local auction saleroom for £22. If the original owner had taken the trouble to have them valued he or she could have given a far more generous contribution to the charity concerned.

Plaques made specially for wall decoration have two small holes pierced in the footrim for the hanging cord. The smoother and neater the holes, the more modern the plaque. Old Victorian rectangular plaques with religious texts or mottoes such as 'Prepare To Meet Thy God' surrounded by a pink lustre border may not appeal to many people today but have great interest for collectors. These are generally referred to as 'Sunderland' plaques because many were made in the potteries scattered around the estuary of the Wear.

Plaques marked MINTON were probably designed and painted in their Art Pottery Studio in London, which operated under W. S. Coleman, a noted artist, from 1871 to 1875. These are by no means common and many were decorated by notable artists.

Fairings

The old country fairs of the nineteenth century and the

bazaars that flourished in the seaside resorts were stocked with all kinds of souvenirs. The Staffordshire figures are well known but little figures and groups made in white highly glazed porcelain are often overlooked. They were made in Germany and exported to Britain in large quantities and are commonly known as 'fairings'. Some were made for a practical purpose in the shape of pin boxes, money or trinket boxes, candle-snuffers or watch holders; others, purely decorative, were intended for the mantelpiece or what-not. Most are of groups with gilt captions on a plinth beneath, often a humorous comment on a domestic situation – 'The last in bed put out the light', 'Returning at one in the morning', or a fairing showing a couple with a child might have the caption 'When a man's married his troubles begin'. Some were adapted from the designs on music covers.

Fairings are keenly sought by collectors: the common ones usually fetch several pounds; the rarer ones may fetch several hundred. So it is important to know what you have. Many were made by Conta & Boehme at Pössneck in Saxony. The earliest have no numbers on the base but by the 1860s numbers were being incised (cut in the soft clay). After about 1880 numbers were impressed (printed by pressing letters on the soft clay) and the firm introduced a factory mark consisting of a shield with a bent arm in armour holding a short sword or dagger. After 1891 the mark 'Made in Germany' was printed on the fairings and those with this mark are the least attractive to the collector. Lidded fairings, mainly for use as pen boxes, which have a group, an anchor, a hand or some other simple moulded motif on the lid, were also sold. So if you have any fairings to dispose of try to get some idea of their rarity and value by consulting the following illustrated books:

Anderson, M. (Editor) *Victorian Fairings and Their Values* (Lyle Publications, 1975)
Bristowe, W. S. *Victorian China Fairings* (Black, 1964/71).

Feeding Bottles

Mid-nineteenth-century feeding bottles for babies would shock most mothers today. They were made of pottery and were almost impossible to clean properly. The milk was poured into a central opening (plate 8) and a teat of some kind was tied to the mouth end, often just the finger from an old glove. These were in use up to about 1860 when the firm of Maws began to make glass feeding bottles, using much the same design. However, it was at least possible to see if they were clean. Today these old feeding bottles, particularly those with blue-printed patterns can sell for more than £25.

Finger Bowls

Finger bowls, or finger glasses as they are sometimes called, were filled with water and placed on the table for use during a meal. They are found in plain or coloured glass, usually with a shallow glass saucer. It is as well to find a practical use for them since they seldom sell for very much. However, do not confuse these with wine glass coolers which are straight-sided, or nearly so. They are usually made of thicker glass and have two lips. Wine glasses were inverted in ice cold water to keep them cool, the stems resting against the lips. They are rather more valuable than most finger bowls.

Hot Water Bottles

Until the advent of the rubber hot water bottle, and still later the electric blanket, most hot water bottles were made of stoneware, flat on the base with an arched body. They were filled at the top and sealed with a stoneware screw top with rubber washer. They sometimes carried printed trade marks. Small stoneware muff warmers were used to warm the hands in cold weather. All these are interesting bygones.

Knife Rests

In the days when the head of the household carved the meat at the table, he had, at times, to put down the carving knife and fork. For this purpose pottery, cut glass, or even silver knife rests were provided so that only the handle touched the table-cloth. The pottery rests would match the dinner service (plate 8). These old knife rests are of interest to collectors and may still be used today.

Goss China

The Victorians were great collectors of all manner of small mementoes which were displayed in corners on their what-not, a piece of furniture consisting of turned posts supporting a series of three or four shelves. It was a habit that lasted well into this century. Each journey to the seaside or to a tourist resort added at least one more item to the collection. Among these were little porcelain ornaments in many shapes, some in imitation of historic vessels in museums, each with a beautifully enamelled coat-of-arms of the town in which it was sold. Between about 1885 and 1914 the craze to collect these spread all over the country, a craze which has now been revived by many serious collectors, over sixty years later.

Goss wares can be recognised by their printed trade mark, a heraldic goshawk above the name W. H. GOSS. The more unusual pieces fetch surprisingly high prices, so do not discard any Goss pieces. The cottages, introduced in 1893, with Ann Hathaway's cottage and Shakespeare's house at Stratford and Burns' cottage at Ayr, sold so well that others were produced from time to time until shortly after World War I. They are keenly collected. Goss wares are sold in the major London salerooms and a good collection can reach three figures. If you have such a collection study it carefully. The following books will be helpful:

Rees, D. and Cawley, M. G. *A Pictorial Encyclopaedia of Goss China* (Ceramic Book Co, 1970)
Ward, R. *Price Guide to the Models of W. H. Goss* (Antique Collectors' Club, 1975).

Goss had many competitors who produced similar mementoes, often in pottery, but none reached his high standard. Nevertheless, these are also sold by bric-a-brac dealers and in some auction rooms.

Lithophanes

You may at some time come across a strange little porcelain panel with a moulded surface no larger than a cabinet-sized photograph lying flat in a drawer. If you study it carefully you will see that the moulding appears to make a picture of such poor quality that you may decide to throw it away. Don't do so until you have held it against a bright light. You may well be surprised. If you see a beautiful, luminous picture, full of light and shade, you have unearthed a lithophane.

The lithophane was invented and patented in France in 1827 but was later manufactured under licence first in Germany and then in Holland and Britain. They were made to be placed in front of a candle or nightlight, or to be hung in a window. By making a simple frame they can be adapted to use electricity as a source of light. Most antique shops will pay several pounds for a really good lithophane.

Match-Holders

In late Victorian times when matches were relatively safe to handle most households kept a match-holder on a desk or the mantelshelf. Many were made of porcelain by the German firm of Conta & Boehme, and some of these are marked with a shield within which is an arm in armour holding a short sword. Several British firms made match-holders of pottery including Doulton and Wedgwood. South Devon firms included them in their output of motto wares. They can always be recognised by the fact that somewhere on the out-side there will be a rough surface on which a match may be struck. Match-holders were also made of metal, wood, glass and papier-mâché.

Menu Holders

In the days of more formal dinner parties with perhaps twenty or more guests it was usual for each person to have a place card and a menu, often designed by a top line artist. Some artistic hostesses designed and painted menus themselves, perhaps combining them with the place card by putting the guest's name in one corner. These had to be placed in a menu holder. Menu holders were often of pottery or porcelain with decorative motifs of flowers or even a printed scene. They are now collectors' pieces.

Moustache Cups

In Edwardian days when gentlemen sported large moustaches, drinking sometimes became a bit of a problem. Some large cups for ordinary use were made with a crescent-shaped china attachment within the cup so that the moustache could not droop into the liquid. A hole in this attachment allowed the liquid to flow towards the mouth.

Pap Boats

These are shallow oval dishes with a tapering spout at one end. Pap boats were used for feeding infants and invalids throughout Victorian times. They were made not only by Maws, who specialised in such wares, but by many Staffordshire potteries. The example shown (plate 8) was made by Mintons.

Pot Lids

The round lidded pottery pots in which bear grease was sold to gentlemen as dressing for the hair were the first to be made with decorative coloured lids. These had pictures of bears in natural scenery or masquerading as humans. As a type of sales promotion they were most successful and were later made for potted meats and fish paste. Since then they have sometimes been framed and used for wall decoration. There are many collectors of pot lids and at least one London saleroom holds special pot lid auctions. They do turn up from time to time in old boxes in attics and cupboards. Preserve them: they are seldom worth less than £15 and rare examples can fetch over £100. Some idea of their value is given in A. Ball's *Price Guide to Pot Lids* first published in 1970 but make sure you see the latest edition.

Lids printed in black with the name of a product such as

88

cold cream (plate 8), shaving cream, or tooth paste, usually accompanied by the maker's inscription, were extensively used in the nineteenth century and even as late as the 1930s. They are all worth saving. A price list is contained in Edward Fletcher's *Collecting Pot Lids* (Pitman, 1975).

Scent Bottles and Smelling Salts

Scent bottles are among the most attractive of small antiques and are widely collected. They may be of cut glass, plain or coloured, porcelain with enamel decoration, or enamel on copper. They usually have a small ground glass stopper protected by a silver, electro-plated or brass cap, either with a screw or hinged. Many were made as toilet bottles to stand on a dressing table and some were fitted with sprays to diffuse the scent. Others were meant to be carried; these are usually coloured glass and are double-ended: two bottles joined together, one for scent, the other for smelling salts. Some heart-shaped bottles were fitted with a chain and ring so that they could be carried on chatelaines.

Smoke Protectors

In the days when paraffin lamps were the main source of illumination the soot from the flame tended to blacken ceilings, particularly immediately above the lamp itself. To prevent this a conical glass was suspended by a glass ring above the lamp. This trapped much of the soot and could be taken down to be cleaned from time to time.

Souvenir China

Apart from Goss heraldic china the sale of small pieces of souvenir china carrying printed views of seaside resorts and tourist centres reached enormous proportions in the last quarter of the nineteenth century. Production began in British potteries even before the Great Exhibition of 1851. A plate with a print of the Thames Tunnel linking Wapping and Rotherhithe which opened in 1843 was one of the earliest to be made for tourists and sightseers. The exhibitions of 1851 and 1862 produced a large crop of souvenir china. The trade reached its peak in the period between 1880 and World War I. In the 1880s various German firms entered the market and flooded Britain with souvenirs of almost every city, town and village in the country. They sold at village fairs as well as at holiday resorts. A very popular type was a plate with pierced rim. These are now known as 'ribbon plates' since a ribbon could be threaded through the holes and used to hang the plate on the wall. They have been called 'china postcards' for they have a similar interest for the collector and should on no account be discarded as worthless. See:

Henderson, I. T. *Pictorial Souvenirs of Britain* (David & Charles, 1974).

Stoneware Jars and Bottles

Throughout the nineteenth century jars and bottles were made from a clay that fired to a rich brown colour and these were glazed by throwing salt into the kiln during firing. This very hard non-porous pottery was known as stoneware and was produced not only in the Potteries and in London but in other centres where a suitable clay could be found, notably in Derbyshire and at Bristol. Large jars were made to carry spirits and other liquors, smaller bottles for ginger beer and other aerated waters, and also for ink. Many have the name of the maker impressed on the surface and, sometimes, the printed name of the firm that sold the liquor. They are well worth preserving as items of local history. Look for the marks of such firms as Knowles or Oldfield of Brampton, near Chesterfield; Bourne & Son of Denby, near Derby, and William Powell of Bristol.

Toilet Services

Before the days of running water every bedroom washstand had its toilet service. An ordinary service consisted of a ewer, basin, soap dish, brush holder, sponge bowl and chamber pot. Large double services had fourteen pieces. Relatively few services have survived intact but a ewer and basin with good colour decoration will now sell well. Many old toilet services are exported to the USA.

Footbaths are also desirable and many of these date back to Regency times.

Victorian Ornamental Glass

Much Victorian glass is very decorative. Cranberry or ruby glass which graced the dinner tables (there is a set on show at Chatsworth House) is much prized today, particularly in America. Many other colours were produced on both sides of the Atlantic and it will always sell for a few pounds. Decanters and the glass bells which were rung to call the maid are more desirable and sell for a much higher figure.

It is important to look carefully at all Victorian glass. If the base has a rough patch in the centre it was almost certainly hand-blown. This is known as the pontil mark. Sometimes it was ground away leaving a shallow saucer-shaped depression on the base. Much Victorian glass was pressed into a mould by machine, particularly after 1870. This can be recognised by the mould marks on the outside, a moulded factory mark, and sometimes even a registration mark (see pp 80–1). The maker's marks include a bird's head (Sowerby's Ellison Glass Works at Gateshead-on-Tyne), a lion erased with halberd (Greener & Co of the Wear Glass Works, Sunderland) and a lion erased above battlements (George Davidson & Co of Teams Glass Works, Gateshead-on-Tyne). White and coloured pressed glass sells mainly for its decorative value.

Watch carefully for any ornamental glass with a matt surface which shades from a flesh-pink into a pale yellow colour. This is known as Burmese glass and was patented by the Mt Washington Glass Company of America in 1885 and was later made under licence by Thomas Webb & Sons of Stourbridge. I had often heard about this glass but had never handled a piece until a neighbour asked me to look over a few things she had been asked to sell for a relative. I looked carefully at a pair of Victorian glass vases which had a peach-like bloom. On the base was an impressed mark. They turned out to be Burmese glass made by Thomas Webb & Son of Stourbridge and they sold for over £300 at auction. They might easily have found their way into a bric-a-brac shop and sold for a few pounds to someone who might have recognised their worth and made a handsome profit.

The Victorians were fond of large coloured glass ornaments which flared at the rim where they were pierced so that clear, prismatic glass drops, rather like those used in crystal chandeliers, could be hung from them. These were known as lustres, and the prisms of glass caught the light. They often look out-of-place in a modern home and are discarded, particularly if some of the drops are missing. This is a mistake: they sell well at auction and can be restored by a dealer in Victorian glass.

Wasp or Fly Traps
Victorian wasp or fly traps consist of a globular clear glass vessel on three short feet with a small circular hole in the top which can be closed with a stopper, and a hole at the base for the entry of the wasps or flies (see plate 8). The incurved hole at the base creates a channel which can be filled with honey and water or some other sweet concoction attractive to the wasps which fly in and, unable to find an exit, are eventually drowned.

Bygones in General

The word 'bygone' is applied to objects which, though useful in their day, have been superseded and now have very little, if any, practical significance.

Bedwarmers
Before the days of hot water bottles beds were warmed by placing hot charcoal in a lidded circular container of brass or copper which was fitted with a long wooden handle. The sheets were 'ironed' by domestic staff to warm them, shortly before the bed was to be used. Such bedwarmers, though no longer used for their original purpose, are valued as wall decoration. Even damaged bedwarmers can be restored.

Bonbonnières
These are small lidded boxes for sweetmeats, shaped in various forms. They were made of gold, silver, china, porcelain and glass. The metal ones were usually embossed with decorative motifs; china bonbonnières were generally painted with flowers.

Candle Snuffers
Candle snuffers are scissor-like metal devices for trimming the wicks of candles. The cutting blade was fitted with a little rectangular box which caught the charred fragments of the wick. The word 'snuffer' is also used for the conical device used for putting out a candle flame. These were often fitted to portable candle holders. Some were made of pottery or porcelain, often in the form of a female figure, the skirts forming the cone. These were made by the Derby and Worcester porcelain factories and are highly prized.

Carpenters' Tools

Many old tools became 'bygones' when woodworking machinery was introduced. They include adzes, axes, braces, chisels, planes and saws, some of which are still used by the few cabinet makers and furniture restorers who work by hand. They are also collectors' items – especially planes which nearly always carry a maker's name and often the name of the original owner. There are several dealers who specialise in old carpenters' tools and a number of museums house collections; one of the finest is in the St Alban's City Museum. See:

Goodman, W. L. *British Plane Makers from 1700* (G. Bell/Arnold & Walker, 1968).

Coal Scoops and Vases

Old coal scoops or scuttles made of brass or copper, sometimes in the shape of a helmet, are worth a considerable amount and even when very badly damaged have scrap value. A wooden coal vase, as it used to be called, consisted of a box with a sloping lid, usually with decorative brass hinges and handle, and a small shovel, sometimes with a white china handle, which slipped into a band at the back. They were also made in japanned metal. Even these will sell if in reasonably good condition.

Brass and Copper Utensils

Although a few cooks may still use utensils of copper and brass these have been largely superseded by aluminium and enamelled cast iron vessels. But brass and copper when kept well polished are highly decorative and many people value utensils of these metals for this reason, particularly the owners of country cottages. Copper kettles, saucepans, marzipan and jelly moulds, brass skillets and chestnut roasters are all valuable.

Corkscrews

Corkscrews are found in immense variety. Many are now regarded as out-of-date and have entered the class of bygones.

Interesting examples are collected. Some have a brush (not unlike a shaving brush) fitted into the handle to clean the top of the bottle before opening; others have various patented devices under the names of such makers as J. Heeley & Sons, Henshall, Lund, Thomason, and Weir.

Curbs and Fenders

In the days when open fires were the rule each fireplace had a fender and fire-irons which rested on 'dogs'. Some were made of iron (known as Berlin Black); others of hard brass or 'antique copper'. The most valuable curbs are those made of pierced brass with brass fire-irons.

Cycle Lamps

Before the use of electric batteries in cycle lamps, they were lit with paraffin or with acetylene gas. The acetylene lamps had a small reservoir of water above a container at the base which was filled with calcium carbide. By releasing drops of the water on to the carbide, acetylene gas was given off which could be ignited, producing a brilliant white flame. These lamps needed constant attention but they gave a very powerful beam of light. They are now bygones. Don't throw one away.

Door Porters

Door porters turn up more frequently in country districts than in towns. Country people working on farms or in the wheelwright's shop were always in and out of their cottages and in warm weather the doors were kept open by using a door porter. They were heavy pieces of moulded or cast iron which could be carried from place to place. Most of them are in the shape of an animal – a fox, a sheep, a horse or even a lion. Many were made in the shape of Punch, a design adapted from the cover of that periodical. Others were made to represent well-known politicians such as Disraeli or Gladstone, or a notable soldier, such as Wellington. Rusty porters retrieved from sheds can be cleaned by scrubbing with a stiff brush and can then be polished with grate polish or even black boot polish. Some porters may have been painted black: this is unfortunate since the paint settles in the hollows and destroys the crispness of the design. If you must paint one, use a thin matt blackboard paint.

Fire Grates
Cast iron was popular in Victorian times and most fire grates were made in this material. They were fitted downstairs and in most bedrooms. Many are still *in situ*, sealed off behind a panel. However, they are sometimes taken out during renovations. Don't send one immediately to a scrap yard or leave it to rust away in a corner. If you advertise it or send it to a saleroom you may well be able to sell it to someone who wants to install one in a country cottage.

Footscrapers
An iron footscraper fitted with a circular or oval dish to catch the mud can readily be sold today. If rusty, treat it as you would a door porter.

Footwarmers
At one time when people travelled by coach or in unheated railway carriages or cars without heaters, a portable copper tank was filled with hot water at the start of a journey. This was used as a footwarmer and, occasionally, one may turn up among other bygones. I have even seen a copper stomach warmer, bearing the name of a hydropathic establishment, which had obviously been made to ease stomach pains.

Grape Scissors and Nutcrackers
The Victorian dessert course usually included both bunches of grapes and nuts in their shells. Implements had to be provided to deal with these. Specially designed silver or plated grape scissors were made to snip a few grapes from the bunch and these were usually highly decorative, the handles with vine leaf motifs. Metal nutcrackers, sometimes with ivory

handles, and small 'pick nuts', shaped like scalpels to remove the kernel from the shell, were also part of the dessert-eating equipment.

Irons and Iron Stands

The electric iron has ousted the box iron and the flat iron yet even the common types will sell today for £1 or more. The more unusual types fetch much higher prices.

There is one type of iron which is not always recognised. This is the gophering iron (plate 8) which was used by the Victorians for smoothing the ornamental plaiting used for frills and the borders of women's caps. It consisted of a hollow bullet-shaped piece of brass or iron, mounted on an iron stand, into which a smaller piece of hot iron could be inserted. This was attached to an iron rod with a wooden handle to hold so that the metal could be heated in the fire as one might heat a poker.

Small irons were also made for ironing felt and silk hats. These were slightly curved pieces of iron riveted to a metal rod inserted into a metal handle.

As a flat iron could not be placed directly on the ironing table, stands of iron or brass were used (plate 8). Brass iron stands can be extremely attractive and are often hung up by collectors as wall decoration. The earliest are of hand-worked brass but, by the middle of the nineteenth century, they were usually of cast brass. Most examples are pierced and there are hundreds of different designs.

Locks and Keys

Old keys should be given away rather than thrown away: many furniture dealers like to keep a box of old keys on the off-chance that one will fit a keyless lock. Really old locks and keys are collected so you may find an antique or bric-a-brac shop glad to have them.

Motoring Mascots

Car mascots on radiator caps first appeared in 1908 and were

97

common before World War I. Some were merely trade marks; others were specially commissioned by car owners and are therefore rarer. Many were designed by eminent artists. The Rolls Royce mascot 'Spirit of Ecstasy', for example, which appeared in 1911, was designed by Charles Sykes, R.A. Most were made of metal but in the 1930s glass mascots were made by Lalique. Collectors of car mascots pay high prices which may range from a few pounds to over one hundred pounds each.

Picture Frames

In many sheds and outhouses an assortment of old picture frames can be found leaning against the wall. Occasionally a quite valuable picture or print may be hidden among the frames. Look out, for example, for old hunting prints. These will usually sell and it is surprising what can be done by the experts to restore them to something like their original condition. What about the old frames? Fortunately, many types of antique frames are now sought after, especially the maple frames of Victoria's reign. They are all the more desirable if they still have their original glass and the narrow bevelled gilt mount with which they were usually fitted. The old small frames of ebonised wood with a circular or oval aperture surrounded by an ormolu or brass rim which were used for small prints and miniature portraits are now difficult to find and fetch good sums of money. They were often fitted at the top with a repoussé acorn and leaf ornament which held the ring for hanging. Then there are fine frames in various sizes of rosewood, pearwood and satinwood which glow with a beautiful patina when cleaned and polished. Watch for them and preserve them for posterity. Old picture frames should be offered to a picture dealer or entered in an auction sale.

Small photograph frames need careful examination. If they are of tarnished metal clean a strip to see if you can identify the metal. Plain ones are often of brass. If you find a silvery metal look carefully for a hallmark which is sometimes very difficult to find on an embossed surface, particularly if the hollows are tarnished and dirty. Silver frames are in constant demand.

Pocket Knives

The penknife on the desk for cutting quills was, no doubt, used occasionally for other purposes. In Edwardian times pocket knives, or pocket cutlery, were extremely popular and had varied uses. There were chatelaine knives, smokers' knives, sporting knives, campaigners' knives, yachting knives, motoring knives, scissor knives, rule knives, toilet knives and engineers' knives. Each would have an appropriate selection of folding implements in addition to cutting blades. A smokers' knife had a pipe pick and pipe stopper, a campaigning knife had a tin-opener, corkscrew and screwdriver, and so on. They varied enormously in quality. A chatelaine knife would be a collector's piece. The handle would probably be of ivory, shell or mother-of-pearl. There would be a silver blade for fruit, a button hook, scissors and small corkscrew in addition to the usual blade. On the other hand many pocket knives were made cheaply as give-away advertising items for good customers. The knife produced for a Scotch Whisky firm (plate 2) inevitably had implements for opening bottles.

Stuffed Birds and Animals

Victorians loved to display stuffed birds and animals mounted in glazed rectangular cases against a background of rocks, ferns or moss. The custom began soon after the Great Exhibition of 1851. The techniques of taxidermy improved during this period and later examples tend to be better preserved, with colours unfaded. Many still survive in attic, shed or workshop. They are now in demand, especially the rarer specimens which were brought back from North America and the East by hunters and explorers. These often find a final home in a museum but even British birds and animals find a market for they are acquired by collectors and interior decorators. See:

Herriott, Sue. *British Taxidermy: A Historical Directory* (Leicester Museum, 1968).

Sugar Cutters

When the Victorians bought sugar it came in large cone-shaped pieces known as sugar loaves and it was necessary to crush the loaf or break pieces from it as they were needed. This was done with a sugar cutter made of two pieces of iron hinged like a pair of scissors. The sharp cutting edges on the end of each blade were shaped like half-moons.

Table Lamps

Before the days of gas and electricity and in country districts where the provision of electricity was long delayed, the paraffin lamp was the main source of illumination in living rooms and candle-holders were still used in bedrooms. Table lamps consist of three main parts – a stand, a reservoir to hold the paraffin which is soaked up by the wick, and a glass chimney and globe to contain the flame and diffuse the light. All three sections can be highly decorative. The stand may be of brass, the reservoir of cut or coloured glass, the shade of tinted opalescent or frosted glass. Table lamps are sought after to convert for electricity, indeed, they are actually reproduced with electric fitments. The supply of old lamps hardly meets the current demand and really good examples sell extremely well. Damaged lamps may well have spare parts which are needed to restore others. Old chimneys and shades in particular are wanted.

Tins

The lidded tin as a form of airtight packaging has been largely replaced by packets covered with transparent plastic. Biscuits, for example, were at one time sold loose from a large tin or ready packed in a one pound tin, either colour-printed or covered with paper carrying a colour-printed design. Old tins, of all kinds, are now collected, particularly those with unusual patterns or shapes. Some were made to resemble books, handbags or clocks. Tobacco was sold in small tins which bore the name of the brand – 'The Quiet Moments Mixture', 'Evening Glow', 'Hibiscus'. Particularly interesting are the tin money banks made mainly for children, often in the shape of a pillar box. Commemorative tins are of special interest (plate 8).

Trivets

Trivets were made for use in front of an open fire and usually consisted of a rectangular pierced platform supported by four legs; some round examples fitted on the bars of the grate to take a kettle or saucepan. Many trivets are made of pierced brass and are extremely decorative.

Walking Sticks and Canes

Walking sticks or canes may range from a rough stick, cut by a countryman from a hedge, to fine silver-mounted canes carried by city dandies. A very ordinary looking walking stick may, in fact, conceal some unusual feature – for many also acted as containers, fulfilling a dual purpose. So examine old walking sticks carefully to see whether the handle or the ferrule is made to unscrew. Some contain a sword, or even a gun, which travellers could use to defend themselves against thieves. Others, known as optical canes, are fitted with small telescopes or lenses. Then there are the smokers' canes with handles containing cigarettes, vesta boxes, or snuff boxes. Sticks for use in dark streets may encompass lighting devices; others have spirit flasks, whistles, pill boxes, sealing wax, pencils or perhaps a map to help the owner find his way. Needless to say, all these can be collectors' items. Regimental canes with crests on silver mounts were produced for most units and are sought by collectors of militaria.

Water Filters

The work of Louis Pasteur and Joseph Lister on bacterial

infection made the Victorians begin to take greater care over their water supplies. Many families began to filter their drinking water through charcoal or silicated carbon. This was done in a large stoneware cylinder fitted with a tap. Many were placed in a prominent position and for this reason were decorated. In the 1880s Doulton's began to produce 'art pottery' filters. Some firms made filters in glass so that the filter portion could be removed and the carafe-shaped lower portion containing the filtered water could be placed on the table.

The list of bygones is almost endless. Only a few have been mentioned. If you come across any old article which clearly had a practical use in the past but which now puzzles you, find out about it, don't throw it away.

Index

Figures in italics denote plates